THE NIGHTINGALE AND THE HAWK

THE NIGHTINGALE AND THE ROSE

THE NIGHTINGALE
AND THE HAWK

A PSYCHOLOGICAL STUDY OF KEATS' ODE

KATHARINE M. WILSON

London
GEORGE ALLEN & UNWIN LTD
RUSKIN HOUSE MUSEUM STREET

PRINTED IN GREAT BRITAIN
in 10 pt Juliana type
BY WILLMER BROTHERS AND HARAM LTD
BIRKENHEAD

CONTENTS

CHAPTER ONE

THERE are almost as many interpretations of Keats' *Ode to a Nightingale* as critics of it. It acts like a personality test, registering the precise degree of difference from him. This in itself says something about the *Ode*; it has taken the stamp of Keats' psychological state at the time he wrote it. To look through the eyes of anyone unlike ourselves is impossible without a very special key, and until now the key to Keats has not existed. But after more than a century that key has come to light in the psychology of Jung. A fantastic correspondence exists between Keats and aspects of Jung's psychology. Jung can be elucidated in terms of Keats, and Keats in terms of Jung. As my interest is primarily literary, I hope to use Jung to elucidate Keats, but since this involves some explanation of Jung for those not familiar with his work, I shall begin by using Keats to illuminate what is relevant in Jung's psychology.

Jung differs from Freud in presupposing a deeper layer of unconsciousness. On his view not only does man have a personal unconscious where all his experiences lie forgotten, parts of them perhaps irretrievably so; beyond this personal unconscious lies a basic psychological activity common to the whole race of man, which the consciousness can never reach. Freud has familiarized us with the idea of the unconscious mind influencing our conscious feeling, thinking, imagination and action. Jung's racial or collective unconscious influences us in a similar way only more fundamentally. It acts like instinct. Certainly much that we call instinctual may be activated by it, perhaps all. Thus the reason why our parents appear quite different to us from any other men and women who are not parent-substitutes, different even from our most intimate aunts and uncles, is because determining factors in our racial unconscious provide for it. These determining factors Jung calls archetypes. We could define an archetype as such a determining factor. In talking of definitions, however, we must realize that our psyches are energies not things, and therefore their qualities can no more be caught in a definition than a portion of a stream of water. We cannot really define our attachment to our parents much less what causes it.

Archetypes remain unconscious. Jung posits them because he has observed their activity, just as gravity was posited because its activity

9

can be observed. We can see them at work not only in such fundamental attitudes as those to our parents; they are also mirrored in
spontaneous images. Archetypal images are common to all mankind. They occur spontaneously as outcrops from unconsciousness.
Thus the myths of all peoples have a fundamental resemblance. And,
more conclusively for Jung's theory, such mythological images occur
spontaneously in the dreams of modern people who may not know
their mythological parallel. Moreover when they occur they have the
same meaning, or indicate similar psychological states, whether they
appear in dreams or in mythology. Thus situations in myths long
forgotten illuminate the meaning of modern dreams.

This is relevant to archetypal imagery in poetry, to images that is,
which come from the deeper layers of the poet's psyche, rather than
from his superficial observation, or from his personal unconscious.
Since, almost by definition, a poet is a man of imagination, his mind
often functions by means of archetypal imagery. It is no figure of
speech to say that the poet makes contact with a universe of imagery.
He has a way into this universe. Or rather, this universe has a way
into his mind. 'Universe' is both an unsuitable and a suitable word
for it. It is unsuitable since it appears that the world of unconscious
imagery is chaotic and uncreated, not unified. It is suitable in indicating a realm inconceivably vast. Astronomy has now revealed our
external universe as inconceivably vast. It is so vast that our consciousness is stretched in the effort to conceive of it. On Jung's view
consciousness is a small area of the psyche balancing precariously on
a vaster unconsciousness. Since even on Freud's view the unconscious
contains the memory of every conscious experience, it must be filled
with images as vast as we have ever conceived. On Jung's view the
chaos of the unconscious must have an immensity impossible to
conceive.

This realm of the unconscious broods over the mind of the poet, no
less than over the mind of each one of us. It spills over into the
consciousness of the poet, and in madness it can cloud the mind of
its victim obliterating everything else. Keats was well aware of both
these facts. Huge archetypal images passed through his conscious
mind. In his sonnet, *When I have fears*, he refers to his 'teeming
brain', to seeing

upon the night's starr'd face,
Huge cloudy symbols of a high romance.

What is on the verge between consciousness and the unconscious is 'cloudy' and indeterminate. This line refers to an experience on the further verge of consciousness. The archetypal is felt as gigantic and dominating. It is the realm not of everyday personal experience, but of the formative forces controlling man's mind. It is the region where God and devil are powers, where the gods of *Endymion* reign. Thus in the hymn to Pan, Keats makes the Chorus sing:

> 'Be still the unimaginable lodge
> For solitary thinkings; such as dodge
> Conception to the very bourne of heaven,
> Then leave the naked brain: be still the leaven
> That spreading in this dull and clodded earth
> Gives it a touch ethereal—a new birth:
> Be still a symbol of immensity;
> A firmament reflected in a sea;
> An element filling the space between;
> An unknown—but no more:'

This is not wild raving, but a precise description of the experience of the archetypal. The unconscious is a lodge for imagery that emerges in solitary thinking. At its furthest this sort of awareness not only takes one to the very edge of heaven, but what is to be found there dodges or evades awareness. When it goes, the brain may well feel naked, left empty. It is the archetypal that gives the dull brain ethereal awareness. From it comes new birth. I shall comment further on this passage in its context, and only add here that it represents an unknown, a point Jung frequently makes. What Keats intended by 'no more' is not quite clear. It may indicate that he has finished what he intends to say, but this seems not quite suitable to end a stanza in a hymn. I take him to mean that the unimaginable lodge is no more than an unknown for consciousness, no more until consciousness can grasp it in some form. This makes psychological sense. Keats begins his statement by saying that it is unimaginable, a reality beyond the grasp of the imagination. So he ends by putting this negatively; it is an unknown, no more, but 'no more' being used without any pejorative intention. It is not surprising that Keats should be aware of the working of his own mind since it must be the common experience of poets. But it is surprising that he should be able to detach himself sufficiently from his experience to analyse and comment on it in this way. If I may use his own image from another context, the anchor keeping him safe in the harbour of sanity was strong.

I refer of course to his *Lines written in the Highlands after a Visit to Burns Country*. He tells us that he had been traversing 'a silent

11

plain' with associations of ancient battles and Druids. He was walking with his eyes 'fast lidded to the ground', and thus lost contact with his actual surroundings. Then he suddenly bursts out, 'if a madman could have . . . a healthful day To tell . . . when first began [the] decay [of his mind]

> He might make tremble many a one whose spirit had gone
> forth
> To find a Bard's low cradle-place about the silent North !

which was his situation at the moment. He comments that only a few steps remain into a region that 'Would bar return'. 'O horrible !' he says, to give up 'Brother's eyes' and 'Sister's brow' for

> a painter's sense
> When shapes of old come striding by, and visages of old,
> Locks shining black, hair scanty grey, and passions manifold.

That is to say it is only a step from poetic awareness of archetypal imagery to madness. But he feels at 'the cable's length' and 'the gentle anchor' pulls and he 'gladdens in its strength'.

> One hour, half-idiot, he stands by mossy waterfall,
> But in the very next he reads his soul's memorial : —

By the last line I take him to mean that he can look on the experience objectively, read it, and that what he reads is the memory of the soul experience he has just escaped from. The anchor pulling him back to normality, returns him to the external world. He looks round on the actual landscape and by letting it absorb his attention, comes back to sanity.

Possibly all poets of intense imagination have similar experiences. Wordsworth suffered a more persistent haunting by archetypal imagery as a boy. He says,

> for many days, my brain
> Worked with a dim and undetermined sense
> Of unknown modes of being; o'er my thoughts
> There hung a darkness, call it solitude
> Or blank desertion. No familiar shapes
> Remained, no pleasant images of trees,
> Of sea or sky, no colours of green fields;
> But huge and mighty forms, that do not live
> Like living men, moved slowly through the mind
> By day, and were a trouble to my dreams.

The child fears such visitations from beyond consciousness less than the adult, not recognizing how dangerous they might be. Sacheverell Sitwell, who like Keats writes a poetry of teeming images, tells us in *The Gothick North* how he sometimes spent a whole day writing poetry but as his nerves could not stand the strain he looked for the sort of prose that would relieve him of such imagery rather than encourage it. Prose gives a safer outlet for the archetypal than poetry because more consciously organized and controlled. Keats ends his poem thus:

> Yet be his anchor e'er so fast, room is there for a prayer
> That man may never lose his mind on mountains black and
> bare;
> — — — — — — — — — — — —
> And keep his vision clear from speck, his inward sight unblind.

When I have fears describes a specific experience of entering the realm of the archetypal:

> When I have fears that I may cease to be
> Before my pen has glean'd my teeming brain,
> Before high-piled books, in charactery,
> Hold like rich garners the full ripen'd grain;
> When I behold, upon the night's starr'd face,
> Huge cloudy symbols of a high romance,
> And think that I may never live to trace
> Their shadows, with the magic hand of chance;
> And when I feel, fair creature of an hour,
> That I shall never look upon thee more,
> Never have relish in the faery power
> Of unreflecting love; — then on the shore
> Of the wide world I stand alone, and think
> Till love and fame to nothingness do sink.

We might paraphrase by saying that when Keats reflects that he might not live long enough to trace the images that fill his brain 'with the magic hand of chance'—a pregnant phrase for guidance by the unconscious—and that death might deprive him of his love, the two things he most desires, then he broods till he feels as if he were alone, standing on the shore or the borders of the sea of the unconscious. He thinks (not with logical thinking, but with the penetration of reverie) he thinks until he becomes aware of the vast mystery of the whole interior and gigantic world, and in the face of that experience his personal love and fame dwindle to things of no consequence at all. The sonnet describes an inner experience of great power. The last lines are explicable only on that assumption.

When I have fears carries its meaning unambiguously if we accept

13

it as a precise statement. But since it is often interpreted on a more superficial level, I should perhaps verify the deeper interpretation from the letter to Reynolds of January 31, 1818 in which Keats quotes it. As he so often does in his letters, he begins with a deceptive lightness. He had resolved the conflict referred to in his sonnet, mastered the fear that he might die before realizing what he most desired from life; and the enlargement of attitude putting love and fame in their right and by comparison diminutive place had brought him peace. He writes therefore in a happy mood. He says he had meant to write a serious letter but it is a sunny day, and Keats' spirits were much at the mercy of the weather. Moreover he is pleased by finding 'a mere muslin Handkerchief very neatly pinned'. So in this gay and frivolous mood he writes some superficial verse and begins another bit of nonsense thus:

> Hence Burgundy, Claret, and Port,
>   Away with old Hock and Madeira,
> Too earthly ye are for my sport;
>   There's a beverage brighter and clearer.

This beverage is poetry. He continues:

> On the green of the hill
> We will drink our fill
> Of golden sunshine,
> Till our brains intertwine
> With the glory and grace of Apollo!

Then in his relaxed mood an aftermath of the experience of the sonnet rises in his mind, and he continues:

> God of the Meridian,
>   And of the East and West,
> To thee my soul is flown,
>   And my body is earthward press'd.—
> It is an awful mission,
> A terrible division;
> And leaves a gulph austere
> To be fill'd with worldly fear.
> Aye, when the soul is fled
> To high above our head,
> Affrighted do we gaze
> After its airy maze,
> As doth a mother wild,
> When her young infant child
> Is in an eagle's claws —

14

> And is not this the cause
> Of madness?—God of Song,
> Thou bearest me along
> Through sights I scarce can bear:
> O let me, let me share
> With the hot lyre and thee,
> The staid Philosophy.
> Temper my lonely hours,
> And let me see thy bowers
> More unalarm'd!

This is to say that the poet's experience is terrifying because it creates a gap between his awareness of his body with its weight and solidity and his mind rapt away in strange archetypal regions. The experience comes near to madness, so high does the eagle flight transport him from outer reality. Since these visions are almost more than he can bear, he prays that he may have 'staid' logical thought tied to the earth to temper the solitude which allows imagination to take control. After this comment on his creative burst the letter continues by quoting 'my last sonnet', which was *When I have fears*. This puts the sonnet into its context. It would not have occurred to Keats in a verse beginning so frivolously to write of this terrifying gap between ordinary experience and the experience of the poet if the contrast between archetypal visions and prose reality were not a recent one, a memory just at the back of his mind.

Among the archetypes that of the Self has a special place in Jung's psychology. The term, 'the Self' was taken by him from Eastern philosophy where it indicates the individual's portion of the divine Whole, or the Whole functioning in the individual. We could translate this into Western terms by saying it is what of God the individual finds in himself. This is a far from good way of defining it, however. The psychological foundation is empirical, based on observation of the workings of the mind. Thus the term as used by Jung is a generic one including all its manifestations and all interpretations of it. The two examples I have given are specific interpretations. On Jung's view it is impossible to define since it is never wholly known. He describes it on several occasions, however, by referring to known aspects. Since the psyche is an activity it is best defined in terms of activity. As an activity, to put it shortly and necessarily inadequately, it is the Whole as it organizes the chaos in the individual. It comprises, in one of the senses in which Jung uses the word, the whole of the individual's psyche. It includes the ego, which is the conscious part of the psyche. I suppose we could say that the ego organizes conscious experience into a unity, the unity understood as 'I', but that the Self also organizes the chaos and impersonality of the unconscious into a unity, at least when the individual becomes aware of it. To become aware of it is to have an experience of oneness, or wholeness. This 'experience of oneness' is, like 'the Self', a generic term. It is experienced in different forms and given different interpretations. One of the best known of Jung's images for the relationship between the ego and the Self is that of the ego as like the visible part of an iceberg with the much larger unconscious part of the psyche like the part buried under the water. The Self is the whole iceberg. Since the ego is relatively tiny it is no accident that Keats who was so aware of the archetypal functioning of his unconscious should be aware at times of the tenuous quality of his own personal identity, and recognize this tenuous quality of his personal identity or ego as something that has a particular significance for poets.

Jung, then, uses the concept of the Self both for the total psyche and also for the archetype that organizes the psyche into a whole. That is to say for the activity itself and for the result of the activity. The illogicality of this bothers some Jungian psychologists. It is not for me to try to unravel it. What I shall be concerned with is Keats' experience of the Self. 'Experience of the Self', like 'experience of God' is a misleading, not to say repellent term. We ought to say 'awareness' rather than 'experience'. An awareness of God comes into the generic class of awareness of the Self. Or if we want to relate the terms we might perhaps say that the Self manifests God since it reveals God's activity in the psyche. Perhaps this is a good way of talking since God can be considered an archetype and therefore is unknowable except through his perceived activity. In any case both the religious man and Jung confuse their terms in the same way. What is meant by an experience of God, is an experience of the activity of God. Similarly an experience of the Self is an awareness of its activity. 'Experience' is a useful short hand expression, justified as such. Keats never interprets his inner experience in Christian terms, although he was aware of some relationship between the two. This fortunately means that not only need I not consider it in terms of religion, but that it is irrelevant to do so. But I think it helps us to understand his references to his inner life, of which he was most unusually aware, to recognize its relationship with what in our age and country is still very commonly thought of as religious.

The most common way by which we become aware of the Self is

through images of it. Perhaps a better way of putting this would be to say that the archetype throws symbols of itself into consciousness. It is in this sense that we can talk of God as a symbol. Jung says, 'The self, . . . is a God-image, or at least cannot be distinguished from one.' This is a difficult concept as we can see by the reaction of many theologians to Tillich's statement that God is a symbol. Symbols of the Self take other forms, however. These may be visual. They may be shapes like the circle with the centre emphasized, or other mandalas like the Celtic cross, when they come into consciousness with power. But the forms relevant to poetry are those of mental images of such diverse things as the sun, a star, a pearl, a diamond, a hidden treasure, a bird, a fish, a butterfly, a castle, a city on a hill, a high mountain peak, a rose and so on. These occur to symbolize it in dreams. They also occur in poetry, where they may seem to be metaphorical. The metaphor as a figure of speech, however, is not a symbol in Jung's sense, for the archetype that the symbol stands for is always an unknown, and one often knows what a metaphor stands for. Possibly, however, his metaphors mean more to the poet than to his readers. The symbolic writing of poets is often misread as metaphorical. Thus *Endymion* which abounds in symbols, among them symbols for the Self, has been misread by many critics because they have not recognized this. They have therefore taken it to be an allegory. And an allegory is an extended metaphor.

Jung makes a distinction between an allegoric and a symbolic activity. He says, 'An allegory is a paraphrase of a conscious content [of the mind], whereas a symbol is the best possible expression for an unconscious content whose nature can only be guessed, because it is still unknown.' He also says in *Psychology and Religion*, 'Symbols are never simple—only signs and allegories are simple. The symbol always covers a complicated situation which is so far beyond the grasp of language that it cannot be expressed at all in any unambiguous manner.' In this sense it is very questionable whether *Endymion* should be thought of as an allegory. One who writes an allegory knows beforehand what he wishes to say and says it in images. It is therefore 'correct' to look for the meaning—a definite meaning. No definite meaning emerges from *Endymion*. Keats did not start with an idea of illustrating such things as the difference between spiritual love and physical love; he did not write to teach that ideal love can be experienced only in the love of one real woman, nor that beauty is experienced not in the abstract but in beautiful things, and so forth. Neither ought we to say such things as that the plan of the poem is chaotic because he does not present his allegory with clarity or that it fails because he has not followed some plan that he had conceived as a conscious framework, or that it rambles on from one irrelevancy to another. The more understanding of critics recognize that to talk in this way is irrelevant, irrelevant because the poem is symbolic rather than allegoric. It is explicable only if we take it as the poet's attempt to make clear to himself his own inner processes and understand it as an exploration on the boundary of consciousness. It has form, but a form determined by its nature as dealing with chaotic marginal experience. It was written by a very young man with a strong intuition that he was a poet with something to say, recognizing that the first thing he had to do was to discover what this was, and that he should look for the answer within himself.

James Caldwell in *John Keats' Fancy* shows that Keats was interested in the psychology of his day, and that modern psychology had its seed in the eighteenth century. He points out that it was Locke who first used the phrase 'the association of ideas', and even more relevantly that what he calls the association 'method' is that used by Keats, certainly in *Endymion*. It may be that all original art has much of this in it since all fresh intuition, all imaginative impulse comes from the unconscious, and Jung holds that the way the unconscious moves is by association. To use the association method is in fact to be guided by the unconscious. Jung has invented the term 'active imagination' for what he put forward as a good plan for letting unconscious activity come into consciousness. *Endymion* has some relationship with it. He says, however, that it involves conscious activity as well as unconscious, being a partnership of the two. The writing of poetry like *Endymion* is such a partnership and whether the conscious or unconscious mind predominates in any particular passage must often, perhaps always, be very difficult to determine. At all events Caldwell points out that the dream method (which by definition is the method of association, although it may also be organized by some other unconscious factor) certainly plays a great part in the composition of *Endymion*. I do not agree with him that there is no plan in two of the books. There is internal evidence of planning in all four, and even a possibility that Keats started with an overall plan of some sort. But he is certainly right when he describes the poem as 'hypnotic and associational'. Not only so, Keats *observed* his mind working in this way. That is as noticeable in *Endymion* and as relevant from the point of view of what I want to say as that he works by association. As Caldwell notes, he knew how the mind works on the border line of sleep. We can see this from his *Epistle to John Hamilton Reynolds*, which opens,

> Dear Reynolds ! as last night I lay in bed,
> There came before my eyes that wonted thread
> Of shapes, and shadows, and remembrances,
> That every other minute vex and please :
> Things all disjointed come from north and south.

They are both disjointed and come on a thread. Caldwell says that this associative method not only characterizes Keats as a poet; he also thought in this way, and hence his preference for what he called 'a life of sensation' over the logical method of arriving at truth. Caldwell describes his thought as 'unchanneled'. Jung's term is 'undirected'. I need not add that recent work on Keats has shown that 'sensation' as Keats uses it would today be more likely called 'intuition'. It is a sort of interior sensation, the experience of thought happening in his mind, happening to him, rather than being directed by his conscious mind.

In associative thinking the point or meaning comes at the end of the process, not the beginning. The logician starts from his premiss and argues from that. The associative thinker does not know the truth he is making for until it emerges at the end of the process. The impulse to it lies in the unconscious, which throws up images and ideas in a riot until the point of it all emerges. When this happens the unconscious urge is satisfied and the process at an end. This is why the artist in any medium so often knows what he meant only after his work is complete, and not always then. We see its workings not only in Keats' poetry but in his letters, where he often begins with some chaff or superficial observations that gradually lead him into deep waters, as I have already noted in the letter that ends with *When I have fears*; this progression characterizes most of his letters where he writes about his poetry or gives newly-arrived-at thoughts. It is significant therefore, that at the end of *Endymion* 'Phoebe, his passion !' explains,

> 'Drear, drear
> Has our delaying been; but foolish fear
> Withheld me first; and then decrees of fate;
> And then 'twas fit that from this mortal state
> Thou shouldst, my love, by some unlook'd for change
> Be spiritualiz'd.'

So the point of the story is that 'by some unlook'd for change' the poet should be spiritualized, for it needs no great penetration to realize that Endymion is Keats himself. This makes a sufficient answer to the query, why all this round about story to arrive at the end? Writing the poem was the poet's spiritualizing process. He set out on the quest in order to discover himself, for he had an intuition that to write poetry this was necessary. This quest we can observe him pursuing not only in *Endymion* but elsewhere in his writing. In Jungian terms this is the quest for the Self, dubbed by him with the unattractive title of the individuation process. Keats began it, in so far as he chose it deliberately and consciously, as a process to educate himself to write poetry. Jung says this is the quest of the person in middle life, from about thirty onwards. Keats began it in the very early twenties because as is usual with the creative artist he was already more aware of the inward activity of his mind than the ordinary man.

As we can learn a great deal about Keats' inner life from *Endymion* I shall make a short study of it. The only authentic comments on the poem are his own. So I shall begin by considering these. On May 10, 1817 he wrote to Hunt that he had begun his poem a fortnight ago. On the 16th he told his publishers that he 'went day by day at my poem for a Month—at the end of which time the other day I found my Brain so over-wrought that I had neither rhyme nor reason in it—so was obliged to give up for a few days.' He says he feels all 'the effects of a Mental debauch'. He then went to live with Bailey in Oxford, where he worked regularly rather than as a debauch, and with interludes of what would likely be partly intellectual talk as a refreshment and relief. He describes the theme to his sister :

> Many Years ago there was a young handsome Shepherd who fed his flocks on a Mountain's Side called Latmus—he was a very contemplative sort of a Person and lived solitary among the trees and Plains little thinking that such a beautiful Creature as the Moon was growing mad in Love with him.— However so it was; and when he was asleep on the Grass she used to come down from heaven and admire him excessively for a long time; and at last could not refrain from carrying him away in her arms to the top of that high Mountain Latmus while he was a dreaming.

It is not difficult to see where he got his being a contemplative sort of person. It makes an important addition to the myth for it shows that Keats gave his shepherd at least this attribute of himself. It also means that he planned the poem as an experiment in contemplation, as an exploration into the unconscious.

In a letter to Bailey of October 8th, Keats says the poem will be 'a trial of my Powers of Imagination, and chiefly of my invention . . . by which I must make 4000 lines of one bare circumstance, and fill them with poetry'. He then justifies writing a long poem by saying:

> Do not the Lovers of Poetry like to have a little Region to wander in, where they may pick and choose, and in which the images are so numerous that many are forgotten and found new in a second Reading. . . .
>
> Besides, a long poem is a test of invention, which I take to be the Polar Star of Poetry, as Fancy is the Sails—and Imagination the rudder.

Each book was to have 1,000 lines. In a study stressing how much Keats was guided by his unconscious, it is important to keep the balance by remembering this. It shows that the poem was not unplanned in some degree for it cannot have been merely a matter of filling in arithmetic, although no doubt this youthful element may play its part. A thorough-going Jungian might note that a scheme of four is very often a symbol for the Self, but to go into that difficult conception here is not my intention. Blackstone in *The Consecrated Urn* gives it this significance and says that each book represents a pilgrimage in one of the four elements, but I doubt it. He finds some difficulty in making Book I an adventure in the element of fire since the only fire he can find is that on the altar and from the sun. In fact Book I is more earth-inspired than anything else. Fourness and the four elements of earth, air, fire and water appear in *Endymion* and elsewhere in Keats' poetry, but I find it difficult to see that each of the four books in *Endymion* is devoted to one of them. In fact I think it a doctrinaire judgment.

In a letter to Haydon soon after he began *Endymion*, Keats said that he had a sense of being presided over by a good Genius which he would like to think was Shakespeare. I fancy not many of us would like to think so. But we need not doubt that he felt some power from his unconscious presiding over him. He says:

> I hope for the support of a High Power while I climb this little eminence, and especially in my Years of more momentous Labor. I remember your saying that you had notions of a good Genius presiding over you. I have of late had the same thought, for things which [I] do half at Random are afterwards confirmed by my judgment in a dozen features of Propriety. Is it too daring to fancy Shakespeare this Presider?

Writing at random implies being led by the unconscious. Any item confirmed in a dozen features must have emerged from the unconscious, for only it can be confirmed in so complex a judgment, since only it has such an involvement of significance.

About this time Keats had fits of depression. No doubt on the Freudian view depression denotes sex complexes, but not necessarily on Jung's. In Jung's psychology depression is a symptom of anything in the unconscious pressing for conscious discovery. In a continuation of the same letter to Haydon Keats talks of,

> the turmoil and anxiety, the sacrifice of all what is called comfort, the readiness to measure time by what is done and to die in six hours could plans be brought to conclusions—the looking upon the Sun, the Moon, the Stars, the Earth and its contents, as materials to form greater things—that is to say ethereal things—but here I am talking like a Madman,—greater things than our Creator himself made ! !

The individuation process involves just such turmoil and anxiety. When Keats set out on his experiment he certainly thought he was preparing to be a poet, rather than seeking his own inner development. But the two are interdependent, indeed at first were indistinguishable. Writing *Endymion* involved him in differentiating attitudes that before were confused. Likewise if Keats had been clear about his feelings and attitudes before he began, he would not have felt the theme to be poetical. Any imaginative experience at all is an experience on the boundary between consciousness and the unconscious. What gives it its imaginative feeling is overtones from the unconscious. It is this numinous region of his mind that the poet explores. The imaginative or poetic aspect of any writing is precisely this numinous quality. In its nature the meaning of even his main symbol, the moon goddess, cannot have been clear to him when he first sat down to write. She is a symbol for an unknown, a symbol that he felt to be seeking him and winning him—in fact a creative symbol. He had to discover what she meant for him. And what in fact she meant was something much wider, more involved, more undifferentiated than he at first supposed. So the turmoil and anxiety he referred to were very deep seated, involving the chaotic background of creation, the use of sun and stars as symbols for greater things. Another detail of his statement calls for amplification. He realized the danger in the course of the individuation process of attributing to oneself a power one may feel working in one, for he breaks off what might appear an expression of enthusiastic self-appreciation of

22

himself as a creator, although it was no more than a statement of fact, to say that he is talking like a madman in seeming to suggest that he could create greater things than the Creator himself. That he thought it necessary to say this shows the strength of the power he felt moving within himself.

Letters written after he finished the poem are more illuminating. On January 30, 1818 he wrote to his publisher about alterations to it, insisting that the lines where Endymion explains that happiness lies in what beckons us to 'A fellowship with Essence' must be included. He continues,

> The whole thing must, I think, have appeared to you, who are a consecutive man, as a thing almost of mere words, but I assure you that, when I wrote it, it was a regular stepping of the Imagination towards a truth. My having written that argument will perhaps be of the greatest service to me of anything I ever did. It set before me the gradations of happiness, even like a kind of pleasure thermometer, and is my first step towards the chief attempt in the drama. The playing of different natures with joy and Sorrow.

His calling it a regular stepping of the Imagination seems to indicate a spiritual advance by definite steps. Any interpretation of the poem must be able to show such steps. I shall have more to say of his emphasis on joy and sorrow. In his Preface to the published poem, he notes that it was written between boyhood and manhood when 'the soul is in a ferment, the character undecided, the way of life uncertain, the ambition thick-sighted.' There is evidence, then, that Keats recognized that in *Endymion* he was working his way through a ferment to a mature conclusion.

I shall not attempt a full study of *Endymion*, or to give an unbiassed impression of it. What I want to do is to show that it records a spiritual progress, and particularly to show some of the more obvious images of the Self in it. This has already been partly done, notably by Middleton Murry, but I hope a restatement in Jungian terms will lead to further clarification and some different conclusions.

Keats introduces each book of *Endymion* by general contemplative matter relevant to it. The first opens with the theme, 'A thing of beauty is a joy for ever'. It is from that angle that he approaches his test. One of the things beauty does is to

keep
A bower quiet for us, and a sleep
Full of sweet dreams.

Its influence is not temporary but haunts us. 'Therefore,' he says he 'Will trace the story of Endymion'. He will start in spring when

> each pleasant scene
> Is growing fresh before me as the green
> Of our own vallies — — — — —
> — — — — — And, as the year
> Grows

so may his story. He prays that winter may not come before he finishes, but that he may end in autumn. We shall see, however, that he will find that the equivalent of winter must be passed through.

After this prelude Keats says,

> And now at once, adventuresome, I send
> My herald thought into a wilderness:
> There let its trumpet blow, and quickly dress
> My uncertain path with green, that I may speed
> Easily onward, thorough flowers and weed.

So he sets out as an adventurer into a wilderness, an image for the chaos of the unconscious where the trumpet of his conscious thought will herald him. He sets out on unknown, uncertain paths and expects not only flowers but weeds. His attitude is typical of one setting out on the inward path of initiation. In the underworld of the Eleusinian mysteries or in the Greal story the adventurer expected to meet destructive as well as creative forces, weeds as well as flowers.

Keats then proceeds to his story:

> Upon the sides of Latmos was outspread
> A mighty forest; for the moist earth fed
> So plenteously all weed-hidden roots
> Into o'er-hanging boughs, and precious fruits.
> And it had gloomy shades, sequestered deep,
> Where no man went;

The forest, like the wilderness, is an image for the unconscious. The fruit of the search, or the golden fleece, may be hidden in it. Keats notes that the moist earth feeds it plenteously, and Jung that the earth makes the fructifying factor in modern man's search. The treasure is often found hidden in evil; hence Keats' weeds. In the midst of this forest is a glade, the very spot for the Self. A dove, the bird of the spirit, 'often beats its wings' through Keats' glade, and a 'little cloud' often moves across the patch of sky seen there. We may note that in the Tarot pack of cards, which is full of archetypal images, and where each suit seems to tell the story of the path of initiation, every ace, presumably the Self, comes out of a pregnant-looking cloud.

> Full in the middle of this pleasantness
> There stood a marble altar.

In his work on the symbolism of the mass Jung stresses sacrifice as the essential element that precedes the coming of the Self into consciousness. So here in a glade, which suggests the containing element of the Self, its magic circle, Keats set up an altar. It is an altar to Pan, the god of nature. On this scene rises the sun-god Apollo, the god of poetry above everything for Keats. Into the dawn, a symbol for the new life, comes a troop of children who gather round the altar. Then out of the wood a procession appears led by 'young damsels' and shepherds, and 'close after these . . . A venerable priest', followed by Endymion. The priest addresses them and calls them to dedicate themselves to Pan. All the inhabitants of the region converge thus on the altar to dedicate themselves, for the search for the Self involves sacrifice and the courage and determination of dedication. His making these beings of his imagination do so suggests a spontaneous and profound dedication of the poet. The Hymn to Pan follows. He is invoked as the god of nature, of man's work with nature, as

> Dread opener of the mysterious doors
> Leading to universal knowledge.

Only the Self can have this universal knowledge. I have already quoted the climax of the passage on page 11 as an instance of archetypal imagery. But here I might add that Keats' feeling for the god of the earth and its fruits, one of which is man, involves an awareness of his own inner life, where also Pan is god. His knowledge comes by what he calls 'sensation', and it leads to his finding within himself a lodge for solitary thinking where it can stay and spread through the clodded earth of his natural man until he reaches a position where he calls Pan 'a symbol of immensity'. This can be nothing else than the Self. To call the Self 'a symbol of immensity' is not a hyperbole. It has an almost text book rightness. And Keats makes its reference to the Self unmistakeable by stressing its all-inclusiveness. He says it comprises everything, the firmament, the sea, and the element between them.

After calling on Pan the crowd raise a shout, and the ceremony done, dance and amuse themselves. Meanwhile Endymion sits with the aged priest, the old man met on the way to maturity in Jungian psychology. It is by no chance, unless the unconscious causes chance as perhaps both Keats and Jung seem to guess, that wise old men and young women are Endymion's guides and teachers, for the unconscious side of one's psyche is the opposite of the conscious. A young man's undeveloped side is his feminine feeling and his ancient wisdom. These are the figures we should expect a man to meet in his inward journey. For a woman it is different.

As they sit talking Endymion and the priest are at length joined by those who 'were ripe for high contemplating'.

> There they discours'd upon the fragile bar
> That keeps us from our homes ethereal;
> And what our duties there :

Keats calls the bar 'fragile' meaning I take it less that life is fragile than that the divine world is shut from us by only a fragile barrier. The duties are concerned with beauty, and lead to Elysium. They each say what they look forward to there. Only Endymion keeps silent, lost in some secret trouble. Eventually he falls into a trance. Peona, his sister, of all 'His friends, the dearest', comes to him. As his sister she may symbolize the feminine in the unconscious where it comes nearest to the conscious man, and therefore the first aspect of it Endymion encounters on his inward way.

> She led him, like some midnight spirit nurse
> Of happy changes in emphatic dreams,
> Along a path

guiding and shielding him from hurt to a little boat in which she takes him to 'a bowery island', where he falls into a healing sleep. When he awakens he expresses gratitude to her.

> He said : 'I feel this thine endearing love
> All through my bosom : thou art as a dove
> Trembling its closed eyes and sleeked wings
> About me;'

In the earlier version of the passage Keats makes her sprinkle him from 'a dark well', give him wine, and offer him an amulet to smell. It is as if she were easing his inward way. In the final version she merely plays on her lute.

> Surely some influence rare
> Went, spiritual, through the damsel's hand;

But she stops suddenly and says,

> 'Brother, 'tis vain to hide
> That thou dost know of things mysterious,
> Immortal, starry; such alone could thus
> Weigh down thy nature. Hast thou sinn'd in aught?'

She asks what troubles him and Endymion looks back on his life of activity and says a new element has come into it. He had a wonderful dream.

> 'Ah, can I tell
> The enchantment that afterwards befel?
> Yet it was but a dream: yet such a dream
> That never tongue — — — —
>
> — — — — — — — —
> Could figure out and to conception bring
> All I beheld and felt.'

It was therefore one of those dreams that are significant in Jung's sense, a symbol-laden one. He goes on to relate how

> 'the doors
> Of heaven appear'd to open'

and he soared through.

> 'And lo! from opening clouds, I saw emerge
> The loveliest moon,'

the great symbol of the poem, which Keats is to explore. It sailed towards him and he exclaims,

> 'Whence that completed form of all completeness?
> Whence came that high perfection of all sweetness?'

This is to say that he has already glimpsed the Self hidden within his symbol, the complete psyche. Moreover he is aware that it is seeking him. We should not say 'it', however, for Endymion feels that it is seeking him as a beautiful woman, hence its 'sweetness', which implies that the Self is not yet differentiated in his consciousness, but hidden within this wonderful goddess. She

> 'like a very maid,
> Came blushing, waning, willing, and afraid,
> And press'd me by the hand:
>
> — — — — — — — — —
> madly did I kiss
> The wooing arms which held me.'

She was like 'A second self'.

27

Jung calls the feminine figure of a man's unconscious his *anima*. She is not the Self, not man's completeness which includes the masculine side of himself as well as the feminine, but the unconscious half of himself met on the way to completeness. I should say, however, that at this stage Keats does not think of the moon as so much his *anima* as his muse, the inspirer of his poetry. He confuses them; the moon seems to be both at once, both his inspiration and his love. This is not inconsistent, or even surprising, for the *anima* is the figure that leads into a man's collective unconscious, and it was by way of poetry that Keats was led there. Moreover the feminine in a man's unconscious is his creative side; hence the reason why the muses are feminine. So it is natural that Keats should not at first distinguish them. His muse seeks him but she is in a cloud with his *anima*. During the course of the poem and before he wrote *Hyperion* he differentiated the two. The muse of *Hyperion* is not entangled with his *anima*. She too seeks the new god of poetry, Apollo, makes the first move to bring him to awareness that he is poet, and helps him to realization of his power, but she does not love him. Keats' muse, that is, now requires not devotion but dedication. We can see the practical result of this psychology in poets. No poet decides he will be a poet as a man decides to be either a chemist or an engineer. The decision is an acceptance of a creative element which he discovers he has. This is true at all levels. Even the adolescent poet, as I overheard one protest, knows that 'You don't learn to write a poem; it just happens'. And so it must be all the way up to Keats. But to begin with, Keats' consciousness of his muse was not clear of entanglements. Endymion's rapturous love expresses the young poet's attitude both to his creativeness and to his *anima*. It is beside the point to complain that it is not always patent whether he is seeking ideal love or ideal beauty. The moon goddess is both his *anima* and his muse in undifferentiated unity. At this stage Keats is unable to distinguish his feelings. The poem expresses a state of cloudy consciousness and should be understood in this way.

After the hero awoke from his dream he felt miserable because of the contrast he found in reality when his life-giving contact with the Goddess was broken. He even, to use Jung's word, 'projected' the opposite of his figure of light onto any 'innocent bird' that 'Before [his] heedless footsteps stirr'd', seeing in it

> 'A disguis'd demon, missioned to knit
> My soul with under darkness; to entice
> My stumblings down some monstrous precipice:

> Therefore I eager followed, and did curse
> The disappointment.'

That is to say Endymion brings to consciousness his bright *anima*, but with it, his dark opposite. It would have brought suicidal despair had time, sensed as the archetypal Mother, not soothed him. His sister with perhaps unusual psychological perception, showing Keats' perception, keeps silent knowing that argument is useless against feeling. Being extraverted, the opposite of Endymion, she at length asks if this is all. It is strange that so noted a man should pine for this dream, strange that he should deny that it was love that troubled him and yet it must be.

> 'What could it be but love? How a ring-dove
> Let fall a sprig of yew tree in his path;
> And how he died:'

All this inner activity she finds strange, and urges her brother to be active.

> 'how light
> Must dreams themselves be; seeing they're more slight
> Than the mere nothing that engenders them !
> Then wherefore sully the entrusted gem
> Of high and noble life with thoughts so sick?
> Why pierce high-fronted honour to the quick
> For nothing but a dream?'

Endymion, so sensibly but incomprehendingly reproved, feels 'a conflicting of shame and ruth'. But he explains himself.

The conversation between Peona and Endymion is obviously a self-questioning of the poet. He asks himself Peona's question, for she is one side of himself, and discovers the truth about himself for his answer. From the letter to his publisher we saw that Keats attached great importance to his answer, as essential to an understanding of the poem. Endymion makes a self-discovery by analysing the feelings which determine him to go on his quest. This is the first stepping towards a truth. It brings the depression Endymion was suffering from into full consciousness, clarifying his attitude and preparing him for action. He says he has always been ambitious 'for the world's praises'. But his hope

> 'Is of too wide, too rainbow-large a scope,
> To fret at myriads of earthly wrecks.'

This is to say that what he wants now has a rainbow scope, the rainbow being a bridge to the realm of the Self, and therefore the wrecks that a wayfarer on the earth fears do not concern him any longer. Peona's appeal to him to do something worth while does not move him for happiness does not lie there but

> 'In that which becks
> Our ready minds to fellowship divine,
> A fellowship with essence; till we shine,
> Full alchemiz'd, and free of space.'

What he seeks is the divine essence of things, the invisible reality, which is the inner reality, the reality in touch with the archetypes and therefore which has a divine quality. Then follows a wonderful description of the goal of the poet, which I shall examine in detail later, here merely noting that the pursuit of beauty leads to a 'sort of oneness' where 'our state Is like a floating spirit's'. This sense of oneness I have already referred to as an experience of the Self. It is the 'sense', that Wordsworth describes in *Tintern Abbey*, of something interfused in everything, that 'rolls through all things'. Wordsworth, however, describes it not as 'the essence' of beauty but as a presence, a sense that he projects onto outer realities, 'the light of setting suns', 'the blue sky' and 'the mind of man'. Keats, although he approaches it through his physical sensations, ends with the 'state' of being like a floating spirit. They are opposite. Wordsworth starts from the sense of presence, the floating spirit side and then locates it in nature. He ends, 'Therefore am I still A lover of the meadows and the woods, And mountains.' Keats starts with the concrete and ends with floating spirit. They analyse the same experience, although they come on it in different ways.

Keats proceeds to say that there are

> 'Richer entanglements, enthralments far
> More self-destroying, leading, by degrees,
> To the chief intensity.'

These are the enthralments of 'love and friendship'. He places them above those of beauty for the 'entanglements' (that is to say the complexes of feeling) experienced in love and friendship are more self-destroying than those experienced in beauty. This is not to devalue beauty. Anyone who proceeds to such a clear awareness of their feelings does not devalue any of them, for devaluing in a comparison is an immature activity, one only half aware. He continues, 'at the tip-top' of friendship

> 'There hangs by unseen film, an orbed drop
> Of light, and that is love.'

30

There could not be a more sensitive symbol for the Self than this. He has penetrated into the unconscious and become aware of the 'unseen film' beyond clear consciousness, and at that spot is 'an orbed drop of light', 'and that is love'. He intuits it as an orb and as light, and he feels it as love. Here are three common symbols, or ways of being conscious of the Self. But though they are common we must not think of them as psychological *clichés*. Keats was not writing words, but using symbols. And symbols are not ideas, not concepts, not words, but experiences. They are common in the sense that permanent outer objects like the sun and dawn and raindrops are common. They are objective images of the inner realm of the psyche.

Keats goes on to describe the influence of this perception. It 'genders a novel sense At which we start and fret'. This is not eastern mysticism where one loses one's identity in the Self, nor medieval of the sort where the Self is met in a cloud of unknowing. However much Keats' identity may be threatened, or self-destroyed, 'in the end', he continues,

> 'Melting into its radiance, we blend,
> Mingle, and so become a part of it,—
> Nor with aught else can our souls interknit
> So wingedly : when we combine therewith,
> Life's self is nourish'd by its proper pith,
> And we are nutured like a pelican brood.'

The ego, or individual identity remains in this fusion as 'a part' of what it mingles with, and which nourishes its life. It is commonly said that mystic union cannot be described. Perhaps this is so when the ego is lost in it, but since Keats' ego is not lost in the experience he has a clear consciousness of it. Any experience in clear consciousness can be described. In fact Keats achieves this remarkable feat here. The conclusion Endymion draws from it is that anyone so nourished is content not to seize their opportunities for action and fame in the outer world. He says,

> 'And, truly, I would rather be struck dumb,
> Than speak against this ardent listlessness :
> For I have ever thought that it might bless
> The world with benefits unknowingly;
> As does the nightingale, upperched high,
> And cloister'd among cool and bunched leaves—
> She sings but to her love, nor e'er conceives,
> How tiptoe Night holds back her dark-grey hood.'

He recognizes that the Self glimpsed in the ardent listlessness of a

31

lowered threshold of consciousness might bless the world with bene-
fits unknowingly. The nightingale is a symbol of the Self, hidden in
the leaves of unconsciousness and singing of love, while Night, or
unconsciousness holds back her hood of unawareness so that consciousness may receive what is usually in the dark. 'Now', he continues,

> 'if this earthly love has power to make
> Men's being mortal, immortal; to shake
> Ambition from their memories, and brim
> Their measure of content : what merest whim,
> Seems all this poor endeavour after fame,
> To one, who keeps within his stedfast aim
> A love immortal, an immortal too.
> Look not so wilder'd; for these things are true,
> And never can be born of atomies
> That buzz about our slumbers, like brain-flies,
> Leaving us fancy-sick. No, no, I'm sure,
> My restless spirit never could endure
> To brood so long upon one luxury,
> Unless it did, though fearfully, espy
> A hope beyond the shadow of a dream.'

This is not, as Keats thought his publisher felt, mere words. They are
to be understood as said—as a precise description, an accurate detailed
conclusion drawn from inner observation.

Endymion then tells Peona that he has already seen 'The same
bright face I tasted in my sleep', reflected in a pool. He has seen her
three times not in dreams but in actuality. Once he saw her when he
came to the cave that was the entrance to Proserpine's kingdom,
which of course is that of the unconscious. Both pool and cave are
symbols for the entrance to the world of the unconscious. Endymion
ends by saying that he will bear his sorrow patiently as he sets out to
find his Goddess.

> 'And come instead demurest meditation,
> To occupy me wholly, and to fashion
> My pilgrimage for the world's dusky brink.'

This is a good attitude in the psychological search. It ends Book I,
where the poet has led unfalteringly step by step to the end of his
preliminary analysis. This is far from chaotic or haphazard writing.
He started his journey because of an impulse from the unconscious
calling him, a vocation. He has glimpsed his goal. He has evaluated
its worth. His hero has determined to sacrifice common sense for it.

It is 'a hope beyond the shadow of a dream'. The goal is beauty; but more it is love, love for an immortal; it is completeness, the Self.

Book II opens with a meditation on love. It begins on the rung of the ladder which the poet reached at the end of Book I. During his preliminary analysis he perceived a richer entanglement than that of beauty and he now seeks to unravel this thread.

The search soon brings Endymion to a common symbol of the Self:

> a wild rose tree
> Pavillions him in bloom, and he doth see
> A bud which snares his fancy : lo ! but now
> He plucks it, dips its stalk in the water : how
> It swells, it buds, it flowers beneath his sight;
> And, in the middle, there is softly pight
> A golden butterfly;

The golden butterfly is the Self. It takes him to where there is a splashing fountain near a cavern's mouth, and suddenly disappears. A nymph rises up in the water, or in plain prose out of the unconscious and tells him that he

> 'must wander far
> In other regions, past the scanty bar
> To mortal steps,'

before he finds his love. Endymion considers how the struggle involves one city gained only to discover another that must be attacked. He comments,

> 'But this is human life : the war, the deeds,
> The disappointment, the anxiety,
> Imagination's struggles, far and nigh,
> All human; bearing in themselves this good,
> That they are still the air, the subtle food,
> To make us feel existence, and to show
> How quiet death is.'

The moon rises. He addresses her ecstatically and asks her help, then hears a voice from the cavern telling him to descend.

> 'He ne'er is crown'd
> With immortality, who fears to follow
> Where airy voices lead : so through the hollow,
> The silent mysteries of earth, descend !'

This is the call that the searcher for immortality in the Eleusinian mysteries heard. Keats, without necessarily or even possibly realizing the parallel, knows it is the way to the immortal love he seeks. He describes the way as neither 'Dark, nor light', but a mingling, 'a

C
33

gleaming melancholy'. That is to say in the half light between consciousness and unconsciousness. At last far away he sees 'an orbed diamond'. It was like 'the sun Uprisen o'er chaos'. These again are symbols for the Self that have a primeval validity. The 'orbed diamond' is the same imagery as the 'globed drop of light'. The sun rising over chaos is a perception of how the Self gives form and significance to purposeless and unrelated instinct. Keats immediately follows, 'and with such a stun Came the amazement', which, if it is not very well expressed, has the stamp of actual experience upon it. Perhaps it is an experience that should not be poetized, for 'the stun' is the reaction of the mortal, of the natural everyday man, who suddenly experiences the unbelievable. It terrifies him since it overturns his settled experience of what reality is like. Endymion penetrates into a temple;

> he well nigh fear'd
> To search it inwards; whence far off appear'd
> Through a long pillar'd vista, a fair shrine,
> And just beyond, on light tiptoe divine,
> A quiver'd Dian.

He explores until

> he sat down before the maw
> Of a wide outlet, fathomless and dim,
> To wild uncertainty and shadows grim.

That is to say he looked into chaos untouched by creation. This is what lies beyond or around the Self. Since Keats was strongly rooted in outward reality, as we have already seen and as he needed to be, he makes Endymion have thoughts of 'self' (that is of his ego, his everyday conscious self) even here and he thought

> how crude and sore
> The journey homeward to habitual self !

Keats always means by 'self' what in Jungian psychology is called the ego. He never uses it to refer to the Self of Jungian psychology, as indeed he could not for it is extremely unlikely he could have met it used so. He uses it in contradistinction to the Self, in fact precisely as Jung uses 'ego'.

The next paragraph begins :

> What misery most drowningly doth sing
> In lone Endymion's ear, now he has raught
> The goal of consciousness?

34

In Jungian psychology the Self is the goal of consciousness. This line is most interesting as showing that Keats was very well aware, even now, that what he was pursuing was depth of consciousness. I said 'even now', but perhaps it is time we gave up thinking of *Endymion* as a part of his juvenilia. Although he was very young when he wrote it he was most unusually conscious of himself. In fact it is this combination that is so surprising and interesting. Here he describes the chaos in which the Self shines as a sun, or the chaos beyond the Self, and how he felt lost in the unfamiliar region. The line continues:

> Ah, 'tis the thought,
> The deadly feel of solitude : for lo !
> He cannot see the heavens, nor the flow
> Of rivers,

nor any other ordinary thing. As Keats often refers to 'solitude' it is interesting to note this association for it. Incidentally Wordsworth used 'solitude' with similar unconscious overtones. Endymion asks why he must bear this sense of isolation from outward realities and retreats 'back into the temple's chief'; that is to say into the Self away from the chaos it has not shaped; he asks Dian where he can find the Goddess he seeks, for

> 'Within my breast there lives a choking flame—'

This flame is the passionate desire for the Self. But he finds this experience more than the human psyche can endure, so he asks to have his flame cooled by seeing his 'native bowers'. He would like to 'o'erleap His destiny', or escape it. But when he got no response but silence, he 'lowly bow'd his face Desponding' in the humility of the devout soul before its creator. The answer to this absolute submission, this complete ego-sacrifice came 'In a long whispering birth', and to its increasing power he continues the quest. Keats sums up the experience as

> First heaven, then hell, and then forgotten clear,
> Vanish'd in elemental passion.

Endymion would have gone 'down some swart abysm', for all this is dangerous territory, 'Had not a heavenly guide benignant led' him; he saw 'panting light' and went towards it. He at last comes to a room where he sees Adonis asleep.

> Above his head,
> Four lilly stalks did their white honours wed
> To make a coronal;

That is to say Adonis is crowned with the four in one, the form of the Self. He is tended by Cupids as he sleeps. One of them gives Endymion wine and fruit, the sacrificial feast, for the equivalent of the high mass is imminent. He is told to feast while he is instructed. Here is the same imagery as that of the feast of the Last Supper but in a more ancient form, one in deeper unconsciousness. The Cupid tells the story of Adonis, and Venus' love for him. Endymion witnesses the awakening of Adonis, and the descent of Venus in a chariot drawn by white doves to carry him to a marriage in the sky. This is an archetypal image, that of the heavenly marriage that makes the climax of the individuation process. It is as a prelude to this that Endymion was feasted. Adonis has to awake from unconsciousness first, then the heavenly love comes to him and takes him to their marriage. The coming into consciousness of an archetype often begins as a distant vision, frequently a vision in the sky. Its journey into consciousness proceeds by coming nearer. The dreamer who sees a marriage in the sky is not himself near integration. He merely receives a far-off intimation of it. This is the first intimation Endymion has; he does not even witness the marriage, although he has eaten the wine and fruit that feasts it.

Before she left, Venus asked Love's favour for Endymion, and told him to go on seeking, that one day he will be blest. So in his loneliness he travels on with hope in his heart. He visits caves and palaces and stands on 'a diamond balustrade' over

> Enormous chasms, where, all foam and roar,
> Streams subterranean teaze their granite beds.

He follows this diamond path that leads through chaotic and kaleidoscopic beauty,

> all so huge and strange,
> The solitary felt a hurried change
> Working within him.

He feels lost,

> for who beholds
> New sudden things, nor casts his mental slough?

Then 'mother Cybele' with 'dark foldings thrown About her majesty', in a chariot drawn by 'Four maned lions' comes to his aid. Perhaps she is man's primal instinct as well as his archetypal mother. She comes with her wild lions in control. She tells him to go earthward and to pray to Jupiter. Keats comments,

He was indeed wayworn:
Abrupt, in middle air, his way was lost;

The heavenly vision must be brought to earth, to reality. In answer
to his prayer Jove sends his eagle, and Endymion flings himself on it,

> Committed to the darkness and the gloom:
> Down, down, —
> — — — he fell
> Through unknown things.

The symbolism of this may be that without a heavenly guide man
cannot find his way in the upper regions. At all events the eagle
brings him to earth 'In the greenest nook'. He wanders through
'cave and cell' in exaltation but asks, 'Alas! . . . will all this gush of
feeling pass Away in solitude?' Yet he feels immortal. He feels he
could snatch his Goddess from the morning. He is in Jungian terms
experiencing an inflation. But it does not last long. 'No, no,' he says,

> 'too eagerly my soul deceives
> Its powerless self: I know this cannot be.'

So he prays for sleep, to dream of her,

> and that moment felt endued
> With power to dream deliciously;

Then he finds a 'mossy bed' and throws himself on it, and there
'Stretching his indolent arms', he finds his love and they embrace. This
is a closer realization of the heavenly marriage of Venus and Adonis.
It occurs to Endymion himself in a dream, but with a goddess, so it is
not quite brought down to earth, and it is fleeting. At length Endymion addresses his Goddess,

> 'O known Unknown! from whom my being sips
> Such darling essence.'

He asks her to stay with him for ever. She says she loves him but
cannot lift him 'to starry eminence', and ends,

> 'Endymion: woe! woe! is grief contain'd
> In the very deeps of pleasure?'

He wakes and strays languidly until he finds himself in 'a sounding
grotto', where he ponders 'On all his life', and concludes,

> 'Now I have tasted her sweet soul to the core
> All other depths are shallow: essences,
> Once spiritual, are like muddy lees,

37

>Meant but to fertilize my earthly root,
>And make my branches lift a golden fruit
>Into the bloom of heaven:

which means that all archetypal essences are meant to fertilize the roots of his personality so that it may bring into consciousness the golden fruit of his love, or more deeply interpreted, the Self.

Now comes the next incident, introduced with a wonderful sense of impetuous waters. I shall quote it for its sheer poetry:

>The humming tone
>Came louder, and behold, there as he lay,
>On either side outgush'd, with misty spray,
>A copious spring; and both together dash'd
>Swift, mad, fantastic round the rocks, and lash'd
>Among the conchs and shells of the lofty grot,
>Leaving a trickling dew. At last they shot
>Down from the ceiling's height, pouring a noise
>As of some breathless racers whose hopes poize
>Upon the last few steps, and with spent force
>Along the ground they took a winding course.

They are the streams Alpheus and Arethusa. The myth goes that Alpheus loved Arethusa, but Diana turned her into a stream so that he could not have her. Thereupon he turned himself into a river and pursued her. The river Alpheus actually flows into a cavern underground, and this is supposed to be the origin of the myth, although such explanations are inadequate since they leave the symbolic meaning out. Endymion sorrows for the lovers disappearing into the gulf, and prays his Goddess to ease their pains. Then,

>More suddenly than doth a moment go,
>The visions of the earth were gone and fled—
>He saw the giant sea above his head.

So Endymion has lost all touch with the world and is in the underworld of the unconscious.

Keats' step in consciousness in Book II came through the heavenly marriage of Venus and Adonis, reflected fleetingly in Endymion's dream with his Goddess. His dream experience brought the heavenly marriage nearer to earth since he himself was involved, although his partner was a goddess. The result when he awoke was to bring him the misery of realizing the emptiness of reality without her. At the end of the book he took another step, for he saw a vision of love for ever in pursuit and for ever denied. That is to say he experienced his own situation in its archetypal aspect. The archetypal lover pursued the vanishing stream beneath the earth with terrific zest. Endymion, frustrated of the consummation he sought, identified himself with the archetypal parallel. It took him down to the underworld of the unconscious, which is the way to the next step in awareness. The significance of that is indicated by the opening meditation of Book III.

Keats begins his third book by railing against men of action who rule the nations. It involves a political outburst, but his real objection to them is that they achieve 'tiptop nothings'. All this valuing of external activity seems to him quite outdated. By contrast the achievement worth aiming at is

> ethereal things that, unconfin'd,
> Can make a ladder of the eternal wind,
> — — — — — —
> To watch the abysm-birth of elements.

The elements are water, fire air. Powers in these elements

> Hold spery sessions for a season due,

and a few of them

> Have bared their operations to this globe—

shaking hands with 'our own Ceres' and fructifying and beautifying the earth. These are creative forces,

> And, by the feud
> 'Twixt Nothing and Creation,

he swears that the moon goddess is the mightiest of them. Endymion now seeks her not as in Book I as beauty, nor as in Book II as love, but as creator. He swears by the feud between nothing and creation because this is the warfare that is waged in the underworld, 'with the giant sea above' one's head.

The journey in the underworld is the best known of all archetypal images for the experience that precedes the birth of the new man. It is the myth of the sun descending into the sea at the end of each day for rebirth at dawn. It makes one of the commonest of the sublime themes of literature, and it is always felt as sublime, for it is imagery that moves man profoundly. It need not always take the form of a descent into the underworld as it does in *The Odyssey*, *The Iliad*, and Dante's *Inferno*. Maud Bodkin has shown that it

39

makes the theme of *The Ancient Mariner.* It is the theme of *The Waste Land,* where it takes the form of our dead and arid present-day civilization. But all myths with imagery of this sort present a descent into the unconscious involving death of the ego when all its values turn sour in the mouth in preparation for a resurrection into a new world with the birth of the Self. So Endymion is about to plumb deeper into mystery, deeper likewise into misery. He enters it on the heels of sympathy with frustrated love, or more particularly by realizing the kinship of his own frustrated love with its archetypal equivalent. This will lead him to fuller consciousness. Therefore he enters the undersea world with his ego-yearning denied—denied, not sacrificed. He is now in the land that T. S. Eliot calls the hollow land, or in Keats' and Jungian terms, that between Nothing—nothing of the ego, and Creation—creation of the Self.

Keats explains what he means by saying the moon goddess is the greatest of creators. When Apollo the sun god sets then she is

> most alone;
> As if she had not pomp subservient;

as if Apollo

> high Poet! was not bent
> Towards her with the Muses in

his heart, as if the stars were not waiting to be her messengers. With 'silver lip' she kisses 'dead things to life'. This was an odd thing to say of the moon. It is the sun, not the moon, that gives life. He means, however, that she brings all she shines upon out of darkness into light. But that he uses these words shows that he is projecting some inward creative factor on to it, in fact that although the imagery he uses in this passage describes the actual moon shining on everything, in the depth of his mind he is really feeling it to be something else, or as he said in his letter, using it for a greater thing than itself.

The situation when Book III opens is that Cynthia and Endymion are weeping for each other. Endymion is at the bottom of the sea, the furthest possible from her. In Jungian jargon (using 'jargon' as a word that sounds so lovely that Coleridge could write of 'sweet jargoning') Endymion is suffering from the opposite of his conscious desire, and this is necessary if consciousness is to widen its sphere. Only if one is aware of the extreme range of feeling can one approach the total awareness that is the Self. But the influence of the moon pierces into the sea. She has sent her creative influence,

A moon-beam to the deep, deep water-world,
To find Endymion.

He 'felt the charm To breathlessness', and when dawn came,

> He rose in silence, and once more 'gan fare
> Along his fated way.

He roams on 'With nothing save the hollow vast' and dead things—wrecks at the bottom of the sea, rusted anchors, forgotten treasure, skeletons. 'A cold leaden awe These secrets struck into him.' He feels the influence of the moon in his heart too, however. He considers how the moon has from his boyhood, and in youth, been everything to him. She was with him in his work, his play, in the charm of woman, and he sums up, 'My spirit struck' a 'harmonized tune' 'from all the beautiful'.

> 'On some bright essence could I lean, and lull
> Myself to immortality.'

Her

> 'starry sway
> Has been an under-passion to this hour.'

This is a feeling for the moon as the Great Mother, the creator and sustainer of life. Endymion has not yet discovered that his unknown Goddess is identical with the moon, who is still 'an underpassion to this hour'. He prays both to forgive his feeling for the other. In Jung's psychology the boy's *anima* is his mother. In adolescence he has to change from the *anima* as mother, to the *anima* as another woman whom he loves. That Endymion brings his feeling for the moon whose kindly influence he has felt in all beauty and in all love, that is to say the moon as mother, into a jealous relationship with the Goddess he loves shows a step in consciousness. His step into recognizing that though he still loves both, his new love is the stronger leads him immediately to the next advance in consciousness.

> At this a surpris'd start
> Frosted the springing verdure of his heart;
> For as he lifted up his eyes to swear
> How his own goddess was past all things fair,
> He saw far in the concave green of the sea
> An old man sitting calm and peacefully.
> Upon a weeded rock this old man sat,
> And his white hair was awful, and a mat
> Of weeds were cold beneath his cold thin feet;
> And, ample as the largest winding-sheet,

A cloak of blue wrapp'd up his aged bones,
O'erwrought with symbols by the deepest groans
Of ambitious magic : every ocean-form
Was woven in with black distinctness; storm,
And calm, and whispering, and hideous roar,
Quicksand, and whirlpool, and deserted shore,
Were emblem'd in the woof; with every shape
That skims, or dives, or sleeps, 'twixt cape and cape.
The gulphing whale was like a dot in the spell,
Yet look upon it, and 'twould size and swell
To its huge self; and the minutest fish
Would pass the very hardest gazer's wish,
And show his little eye's anatomy.
Then there was pictur'd the regality
Of Neptune; and the sea nymphs round his state,
In beauteous vassalage, look up and wait.
Beside this old man lay a pearly wand,
And in his lap a book, the which he conn'd
So stedfastly, that the new denizen
Had time to keep him in amazed ken,
To mark these shadowings, and stand in awe.

The old man appears in a very undifferentiated state, enveloped in
sea-symbols; that is to say clouded over by unconscious wisdom. True
to his nature he reads wisdom from a book—a book Endymion has
not yet read. He has been waiting for ages in the depth of the unconscious sea for Endymion to come. He exclaims,

'Thou art the man ! Now shall I lay my head
In peace upon my watery pillow : now
Sleep will come smoothly to my weary brow.'

He says that now he will be young again 'stung With new-born life!'
Endymion is terrified. It is interesting that Jung says that the ego is
terrified of what it will find in the unconscious. Endymion fears he
will be torn piece-meal, or burnt up. He panics. He thinks he will
shout for help, but realizes he cannot escape. So he must accept the
situation. He says,

'I must stoop
My head, and kiss death's foot. Love ! Love, farewell !'

However, he puts on a brave show, walks to the old man and 'Look'd
high defiance'. But

Lo ! his heart, 'gan warm
With pity, for the grey-hair'd creature wept.

Endymion is conscience-stricken that he should 'blindly' or in uncon-

42

sciousness, cause the old man to weep. He kneels in penitence. The old man knows his 'inmost bosom', however, and says,

> 'hadst thou never lov'd an unknown power,
> I had been grieving at this joyous hour.'
> — — — — — —
> So saying, this young soul in age's mask

went with Endymion on his pilgrimage. I take it he is young because newly born in Endymion's consciousness, but old as wisdom is old. In fact as the old man tells his story he says he is one thousand years old.

In literary text-book terms Keats has added the myth of Glaucus to that of Endymion. But that is not to tell us much about *Endymion*. Keats added the myths of Venus and Adonis, of Alpheus and Arethusa too, and the story of Endymion itself is a myth. But from Keats' whole treatment we might just as well take them to be his own invention. We need to see why he selected just those out of his wide knowledge of myth. They had seized on his imagination in youth and fructified in his unconscious. In the inward pilgrimage which the poem expresses myths relevant to it suggest themselves. We need to ask why such a myth as this should have been associated in Keats' imagination with the story of Endymion. The reason is that it appears as the most apt symbol to bring his unconscious development to mind. The myth of Glaucus takes many quite different forms, although this need not mean that Keats knew them all. He used the one he knew that was most relevant to his deeper purpose and he altered it where it did not suit his purpose. In the version he chose Glaucus was a fisherman. Keats makes him 'a lonely youth on desert shores'. The 'crown' of all his life 'was utmost quietude'. He loved to 'lie in cavern rude', waiting 'whole days for Neptune's voice', and if it came he rejoiced. But, fool that he was, he 'began To feel distemper'd longings' to have the freedom of all Neptune's kingdom. He plunged to the deep and found he had that freedom. But he fell in love with Scylla, who was too timid to return his love. At last, frustrated, he left his pursuit of her and wooed Circe, the 'arbitrary queen of sense' and as 'a tranced vassal' to her forgot Scylla. At the inevitable conclusion when he saw what Circe had done with the men who loved her, he felt revolted. In revenge she transformed him into a decrepit old man to live under the sea for a thousand years. We might think that the old man of wisdom of Jungian psychology would not have this history. But it suits Keats' story that his man of wisdom should have the knowledge that both he and Endymion, with their complete absorption in heavenly love, lacked, since the unconscious is made up of what the conscious side of the personality lacks. Glaucus brings to the poet's consciousness the knowledge of sensual passion and its ruinous effect in turning men to beasts.

Glaucus continues the story of his wanderings under the sea until he says,

> Upon a dead thing's face my hand I laid;
> I look'd—'twas Scylla !

One day he found a scroll in the hand of an old drowned man who had come in a ship with a suggestion of the coming of the Self. It told him that he would not die after his thousand years

> *'If he utterly*
> *Scans all the depths of magic, and expounds*
> *The meanings of all motions, shapes and sounds;*
> *If he explores all forms and substances*
> *Straight homeward to their symbol-essences;*
> *He shall not die. Moreover, and in chief,*
> *He must pursue this task of joy and grief*
> *Most piously;— all lovers tempest-tost,*
> *And in the savage overwhelming lost,*
> *He shall deposit side by side, until*
> *Time's creeping shall the dreary space fulfil:*
> *Which done, and all these labours ripened,*
> *A youth, by heavenly power lov'd and led,*
> *Shall stand before him; whom he shall direct*
> *How to consummate all. The youth elect*
> *Must do the thing, or both will be destroy'd.'*

So Keats' Glaucus is the old man of all wisdom who 'explores all forms and substances Straight homeward to their symbol-essences'. That is to say perceives the archetypal truths that all forms and substances are particular examples of. There can be no doubt that he is the wise old man of Jungian psychology. Moreover he has the particular wisdom of the poet who explores 'symbol-essences' or archetypes. Keats has used this word to mean precisely what Jung means by archetypes. Glaucus must also bring all lovers who have been separated together and lay them side by side. This is most interesting symbolism. Incidentally, in his autobiography Jung records a somewhat similar dream of his own. He shows in *Psychology and Alchemy* that one of the images dominating the thought of the alchemists was the goal of the heavenly marriage, an example of which we saw in that of Venus and Adonis. He describes the problem as the union of the opposites of male and female in the psyche. So the task that

44

Glaucus was set in Keats' unconscious was the task of bringing his masculine and feminine sides together. Glaucus takes Endymion where the corpses of lovers lie side by side with only the possibility of renewed life. And only with the help of Endymion can they be brought to life and have their union consummated. In other words, only with the aid of the poet's consciousness can this be achieved. When Endymion hears this he exclaims,

'We are twin brothers in this destiny !'

This could be an expression from Jung's writings, for he constantly, both by implication and expressly, makes the point that to win the goal of the individuation process consciousness must work with the unconscious. He says they are twins, and Siamese twins at that. What Glaucus has shown Endymion is an archetypal vision of the individual's task, for in a huge cavern he sees all separated lovers lying side by side—the individual's task in a gigantic form; that is to say in an archetypal form. Just as a vision in the heavens may be the first intimation of something that must eventually be realized on the very diminished scale of the individual's actual life, so too this archetypal vision of Endymion's task in its gigantic form must eventually be realized in his diminished personal experience.

Glaucus now tears 'his scroll in pieces small', a very ancient symbol for making conscious. He does it uttering 'some mumblings funeral', as is suitable. He then winds 'his dark blue cloak' round Endymion, again an ancient symbol for entering the womb ready to be born again. Incidentally Jung says that blue is the colour for the Self. He strikes 'His wand [a womb symbol] against the empty air times nine', symbols familiar to anyone with any knowledge of fairy tales. He makes Endymion unwind a tangled thread to a clue—which is what psychologists do in analysis—and when this is done exclaims,

'The spite of hell is tumbling to its grave,'

as it must at every resurrection, or spiritual rebirth. He breaks his wand, as no one need be reminded that Prospero did. After this Endymion strews 'These minced leaves' on Glaucus and scatters them over all the dead lovers. The old man is transformed into a youth. Scylla comes to life. Endymion 'left them to their joy'. So on he goes to lover after lover.

Death felt it to his inwards :— —
Death fell a weeping in his charnel-house.

The first thing they all do after their resurrection is to go in joyous procession to the palace of Neptune to pay piety. As they proceeded 'diamonds gleams, and golden glows Of amber' fell on them. The entrance to the palace was a rainbow arch and a golden gate. And when it opened the light was like 'the first sunrise'. Rainbow, gold and sunrise are symbolic of the approach to the Self. By Neptune's right side stood Love and on his left Beauty, all three clearly different-iated by this stage in the poem

> there did spring
> From natural west, and east, and south, and north,
> A light as of four sunsets, blazing forth
> A gold-green zenith 'bove the Sea-God's head.

The description rises to a climax with

> blaze
> Of the dome-pomp reflected in extremes
> Globing a golden sphere.

Practically every detail is symbolic of the Self.

After Neptune raises his hands in blessing over Glaucus Venus commiserates with Endymion who alone does not share in this consummation; she tells him to 'wait a while expectant', and to visit Cythera, the moon. Endymion kneels to receive this message.

> Meantime a glorious revelry began
> Before the Water-Monarch.

After the rejoicing 'All suddenly were silent' in preparation for a hymn to Neptune,

> 'Brother of Jove, and co-inheritor
> Of Elements!'

They also sing to his companions, Cytherea, 'white Queen of Beauty' and to Cupid, god of Love. Suddenly Oceanus enters, the even more ancient father of the sea than Neptune. He comes

> To take a latest glimpse at his sheep-fold,
> Before he went into his quiet cave
> To muse for ever—

This signifies that the reign of childhood's unconsciousness is quite gone.

> The palace whirls
> Around giddy Endymion; seeing he
> Was there far strayed from mortality.
> He could not bear it—shut his eyes in vain;
> Imagination gave a dizzier pain.

He thinks he is dying and prays Venus to help, asking where his 'lovely mistress' is. He hears her voice and falls at Neptune's feet asleep. He hears her saying,

> 'Tis done—
> *Immortal bliss for me too hast thou won.*

He awakes on earth.

I hope I have shown how Jungian psychology makes this book not only intelligible, but brings out its design. Keats is far from just filling in his 4,000 lines by adding other myths to his original. The myths of Venus and Adonis, of Arethusa and Alpheus, of Glaucus are those relevant, and indeed, essential to further his progress in consciousness. The story could not develop without them. If Keats had not used these ready-made myths, he would have had to 'invent' similar ones. They are his aids to awareness. With their help he has gone step by step to a fuller understanding of himself. Thus the reason the poem does not end here is not merely that Keats set himself to make a fourth book. The search for the Self does not end with its consummation in the unconscious, however sublime the vision. To leave it there would be abortive. The archetypal vision has to be translated into one's personal life. The union that took place in the undersea palace of the Self must find its counterpart in conscious reality. Endymion is now ready for the final book, where the effect of his inner development will influence his life in common day.

Before I deal with the last book, I think I should note the deeply religious attitude of *Endymion*. It is not just that the hero prays to the gods for help, nor that he has fallen in love with a goddess, nor that his wanderings take place in the archetypal realm, which is the realm of the divine. His attitude is one of constant submission to the gods. When he finds himself in misery or denied, he accepts it. When the lovers are united their first act is to go to Neptune and hymn their devotion and thanksgiving. The whole attitude is one of reverence for the gods and a sense of utter dependence on them. And none of this is done from a sense of duty. 'Ought' does not enter into the poem. All springs from spontaneous ardour. That is to say, all springs from life-giving unconscious impulse. Keats' religion pours into him from his unconscious roots, it nourishes his imagination and personality. His is religious feeling at its intensest, something to which he gave himself spontaneously and wholly, in ecstasy and in utter misery, and not less because he rejected the beliefs and conventions of the Christian Churches as outworn superstition. Nor is this vague feeling. His conscious mind accepts it, and he understands it. The third book has for its theme, creation, which shows that he knew what his imagination was doing, that it was bringing the creation of the Self to awareness. The last book leads up to this for its climax. *Endymion* is far from being the incoherent writing it is often considered. It moves to its goal with a sure instinct.

Book IV opens with an apostrophe to the muse of Keats' native land, in which he says she waited long in silence while the muses of the older world spoke. But she has inspired great poets. When he thinks of them he does not dare to ask for her inspiration, but moves 'to the end in lowliness of heart'. Keats has a feeling of the archetypal as being ancient, and concerned with the old gods. So when Endymion leaves the world of the archetypal and returns to common day, he, as it were, changes his muse to the modern English one. He has been inspired hitherto by an ancient muse. The realm she has given him knowledge of is that of the Greek gods. Now he must be inspired to talk of life in the world of common experience.

Endymion's relationship with a real woman, the home-sick Indian Maid, makes the theme of this book. He has stepped on from concern with his archetypal mother and his Goddess to the next phase in his development. When the book opens he is offering vows 'to heaven's airy dome', which suggests that it is now empty. Indeed there is almost a mocking tone in his statement; he offers 'a hecatomb of vows'. This is true to psychology, for one tends to devalue an attitude that one is struggling to supersede. His vows are interrupted by hearing the Indian Maid bewailing her exile.

> Whereupon he bows
> His head through thorny-green entanglement
> Of underwood,

which may be symbolic of his boy-hood entanglement with his mother. He listens as she bewails that no one is there to love her. The poet intervenes to advise him to flee for 'Phoebe is fairer far'. In this conflict between his dream love and the reality, Endymion leans on a bough wretched. He calls out,

> 'Goddess! I love thee not the less : —
>
> — — — —
>
> For both, for both my love is so immense,
> I feel my heart is cut for them in twain.'

He springs 'from his green covert', an image, perhaps, for release from his mother and dreams. He tries to speak, apologizes for his intrusion but says he is

> full of grief—
> Grief born of thee, young angel ! fairest thief !
> Who stolen hast away the wings wherewith
> I was to top the heavens. Dear maid, sith
> Thou art my executioner, and I feel
> Loving and hatred, misery and weal,
> Will in a few short hours be nothing to me,
> And all my story that much passion slew me;
> Do smile upon the evening of my days :

He has made the step to reality; but the bonds of his past still hold him. The maid cannot understand his dilemma. At last,

> 'Dear lady,' said Endymion, ' 'tis past :
> I love thee !'

The Maid sings a ditty to Sorrow, in which she says that she is like one 'Cheated by shadowy wooer from the clouds'. So hers was a parallel situation with Endymion's. She too had developed, however, for as she sat sorrowing a rout of Bacchus came revelling and she joined them. In this she differed from Endymion who never wavered in his loyalty to his shadowy lady. The Indian Maid sought super-ficial distractions. But after roaming over the earth with the crew of Bacchus she has strayed away from them. She now knows that it is not pleasure she wants. She accepts sorrow now, 'sweetest sorrow'. In the letter of Keats already quoted he said his poem was partly an illustration of how different temperaments react to joy and sorrow. Perhaps he is thinking of their different reactions here, Endymion thrown sky high in ecstasy or falling into uttermost misery, ex-periencing extremes without ballast, the Indian Maid running away from her experience, but finally coming back to accept it. She accepts it perhaps sentimentally. 'Sweetest' is hardly the word to apply to sorrow. Endymion travelled through Hell to find his Self. What precisely she finds by accepting sorrow is not quite clear. She asks if sorrow borrows (possibly for the rhyme) the natural pink from 'vermeil lips' to make white roses blush or to tip daisies, the lustre from 'a falcon-eye' to give glow-worms light or crest the waves in moonlight, songs of mourning for the nightingale. She says she would like to escape from sorrow, but 'she is so constant and so kind'. All the aspects of nature imagined as receiving these beauties are things that moved Keats—roses, pink-tipped daisies, glow-worms and nightingales. She may feel that the Great Mother Earth, who is 'so constant and so kind' deprives her of love, as she could. This may well be the unconscious significance behind Middleton Murry's explanation. He sums it up: 'By virtue of the liberation from Self [read ego] which the spirit of Beauty works in him by love which it awakens,' Keats 'becomes part of the all-pervading, all-sustaining creative power.' This would be to say that Keats remained immature, not having cut the umbilical cord that bound him to his creative mother. There is certainly some truth in this, but Keats appears too mature for it to be the whole meaning. Murry likewise does not take into account Keats' dramatic interest. It is the Indian Maid who sings the ditty, not Endymion. Unless Keats was thinking of the Indian Maid as a contrast to Endymion it is difficult to see what he referred to in his statement that he presented different temperaments in joy and sorrow. The song to sorrow could also be interpreted as meaning that what sorrow takes she gives back by making one sensitive to beauty in nature. It could also mean that what she takes is given back in symbols of the Self, for the rose, the daisy, the glow-worm and the nightingale might all be that. The Maid arrives at the stage where she is 'quite dead to every worldly thing', which is to say that she arrives at the death of the ego, and consequently she may feel that sorrow has given beauty to symbols of great value. If so she has come by her own route to where Endymion has arrived. This is how I take it.

Keats was fascinated by the opposites of joy and sorrow. He seemed almost to feel them entities in themselves rather than aspects of feeling. He was not masochistic; pain gave him no pleasure. His most natural desire was to escape it. He hated ill health, and as he said, was all for 'cutting it'. But he accepted sorrow and pain as equal intensities with joy. And he judged the quality of living by its intensity. He presented Endymion's journey almost entirely in terms of ecstasy and misery, and from the remark about joy and sorrow in his letter we see that this made part of his conscious plan for the poem. His attitude developed as the poem proceeded. The Indian Maid's song expressed a stage in that development. Her song may be taken as a prelude to the next illumination in the poem, the next step in consciousness. Sorrow high-lights beauty at least; at most it tips objects that can reflect the Self.

One of the experiences that Jung emphasizes as a necessary precursor of the experience of the Self as the end of the individuation process is an experience of what he calls 'the opposites', such opposite tendencies in one's nature as hate and love, sensuousness and spirituality. A capacity for intense experience of one implies a capacity for intense experience of the other. We tend to indulge one and deny the other. But a fully conscious man recognizes that his capacity for both is equal, and he experiences both equally. Jung's point is that in moments of perception of the truth, moments we cannot endure for long, we may be crucified between the two. It makes one of the most agonizing of all experiences since in it we are torn in opposite directions by sides of our nature that are equally strong. He takes Christ on the cross between two thieves as the archetypal symbol for this crucifixion. What is interesting about Keats' feeling for joy and sorrow is that they seem to act as opposites in this sense. But one can hardly call joy and sorrow opposite tendencies in one's nature, or can one? They are qualities of feeling rather than contradictory tendencies like hate and love. No moral contrast is involved in the opposites of joy and sorrow at least in Keats' early attitude, although a moral aspect appears later. Perhaps I should leave it at that. On the other hand if we consider Wordsworth and Coleridge as influences in his development, and Wordsworth at least influenced him greatly, they had a philosophy of the inherent goodness and joyfulness of nature. Rousseau's noble savage was behind their philosophy. The weakness of the noble savage is his complete goodness and joyfulness. If Keats accepted this without giving it thought, if he accepted joy as nature, joy as goodness, then one can see why pain and sorrow should be felt strongly as the great destructive force in opposition to joy as creator. Wordsworth and Coleridge when first faced with this opposite fell into a depression they could not really cope with. It destroyed their poetic creativeness. Wordsworth's intimations of immortality are those of childhood experience. When sorrow enters his citadel a glory passes away from the earth. Coleridge summarizes the attitude well in *Dejection: an Ode*, when he asks wherein consists 'This light, this glory', and answers that Joy

> is the spirit and the power,
> Which wedding Nature to us gives in dower
> A new Earth and new Heaven,
> — — — — — —
> Joy is the sweet voice, Joy the luminous cloud—
> We in ourselves rejoice !

If Keats assumed this, then joy and sorrow would mean to him not just aspects of feeling. They would imply wholly different worlds. Sorrow would imperil a philosophy; a world view would be shattered by it. But he does not seem to feel this. His own experience could have led him to no such theory. Yet he was much influenced by Wordsworth, and Rousseau's thinking had permeated the thought of his age. It is clear that joy and sorrow, their opposition, and their relationship were constantly in his mind. Only once does he seem to feel that pain threatens a world of happiness. It comes in a letter I shall discuss later, where he says that to allow one's imagination to dwell on the horrors of nature is a 'flaw in happiness', as if happiness represented an attitude one ought to have, or a transcendent reality.

At all events the Indian Maid's *Song to Sorrow* begins a long stride in consciousness which will be taken in Book IV. Endymion has learnt of the Heavenly Marriage of Venus and Adonis, helped to awaken the lovers in the underworld, married his Goddess in dream, experienced all the miseries involved by his seeking in the realm of the archetypes. It is now time for him to carry this development into his conscious life. The Indian Maid too is ready for it. When they meet, both must bring their desire for love down to earth in sorrow. It is possible, Keats seems to show, to love a goddess in a dream world in ecstasy, where the only misery she can inflict is to leave one. But in actual life, to love is not to live in perpetual bliss. The Indian Maid is human; part of her humanity consists in singing a ditty of sorrow. Endymion is attracted to her not as a goddess, but in compassion. To love a human being involves sorrow not just when that love is denied, but in the actual loving, in her presence and in the experience of love. It is therefore a situation where suffering is of a quite different sort from archetypal misery. The descent from joy and sorrow experienced with a goddess involves a descent in feeling. Keats will now explore this. Endymion must traverse similar situations to those he experienced with his goddess, but with a mortal woman. His love starts instantly and spontaneously, but in conflict with himself and with a feeling of pity for her. He recognizes a kinship with her quite different from his relationship with his goddess. She has trod the same path as he has. They have both come out of the archetypal world of the imagination where emotion is felt in godlike extremes, and meet as equals in the saddened little perplexed world of mortals, drawn to each other in compassion. This is a long step to truth out of dreamland into the unglorified light of common day. The situation makes an interesting contrast with the attitudes of Wordsworth and Coleridge when they are forced out of their archetypal bliss. Keats finds a solution.

Endymion begins by asking the Indian Maid to

> 'gently murder half my soul, and I
> Shall feel the other half so utterly !—

—   —   —   —

> And whisper one sweet word that I may know
> This is this world—'

But he hears a voice from the empyrean crying,

> *Woe!*
> *Woe! Woe to that Endymion! Where is he?*—

He has so lost stature since he was a being who loved a goddess that he has disappeared from that world. He therefore feels guilty. He has failed his Goddess. Mercury, messenger of the Gods, appears. Two jet-black steeds come out of the turf, and Endymion mounts his love on one and sits the other himself. This appearance of black steeds from the turf reminds us of Pluto appearing from a flower, seizing Persephone and carrying her into the underworld. We are now to see what lies in the unconscious of these two. They fly high as eagles, 'Far from the earth' into a heavenly reality. Then a strange thing happens.

> There is a sleepy dusk, an odorous shade
> From some approaching wonder,

and the steeds tire, 'Dying to embers from their native fire !' A mist curls round them. It is the god, Sleep, coming for the first time out of 'the old womb of night.' That is to say there is a lowering of their consciousness beyond the usual threshold. Sleep comes because a dream has told him that at Jove's throne a mortal is about to 'win An immortality'. The statement could not be more precise : Endymion is about to experience the Self, not in a dream but in actuality. The

> raven horses, though they foster'd are
> Of earth's splenetic fire,

stop and Endymion and his lady sleep. He dreams he is on Olympus about to meet 'His very goddess'. He springs towards her, wakens and beholds 'his very dream', but when 'Too well awake' he is perplexed to find not his Goddess, but his mortal love by his side. He finds he loves both, and 'all his soul was shook'. 'Would I were whole in love !' he cries.

What is this soul then? Whence
Came it? It does not seem my own, and I
Have no self-passion or identity.
Some fearful end must be: where, where is it?
By Nemesis, I see my spirit flit
Alone about the dark—

This is interesting in view of Keats' statement of the poet having
no identity, and of his consequent 'Negative Capability'. Keats
here gives 'self-passion' as the equivalent of 'identity'. Indeed
'identity' is used to particularize 'self-passion'. Since he uses 'self'
for 'ego', this means that Endymion feels that he does not originate
his own feelings, which is true of the ego, for we cannot choose
how we feel. Endymion experiences the dilemma of being torn in
opposite directions. He holds two contradictory feelings in consciousness at once, and finds it terrifying. His fear is very like the
terror of archetypal domination that Keats expressed in his lines
about travelling in Burns' country and in *Hence Burgundy*, which
I have already discussed. So his experience of having no identity is
really an experience of autonomous activity within himself; he
feels taken control of by contrary influences. Jung makes precisely
this point, that archetypes like the *anima* are not within man's
control but autonomous. Keats in so far as he is detached from his
inner workings, that is to say in so far as he is conscious, knows
that he is not master in his own house. This is what he makes
Endymion feel. 'Would I were whole in love!' he says. The experience leads him to ask the most fundamental of questions, 'What
is this soul? Whence came it?'—a question that follows inevitably
from recognizing autonomous activities going on within one's psyche.

Although archetypal domination could frighten Keats, it must
have had a positive value as well. If consciousness can hold the
colossal content that imagination feeds it with, it must be in some
sort both enlarged and strengthened by it. The man of great imagination, if he is not swamped, must develop qualities of mind that
stand him in good stead in situations unconnected with his art.
Keats was no Stanley Spencer, unadjusted to external realities. He
did not live in his archetypal world. He was no oddity. It is in the
background of his life. But it had consequences which he noted. He
described the state of his mind when his archetypal activity stopped
as 'naked'. This must mean that when not filled with such imagery
it felt empty of everything. In a 'naked' state his mind filled with
whatever happened to be before his eyes—a sparrow pecking, as he

54

says to Bailey in his letter about negative capability. Or if he was among people whose conversation revealed a different sort of mental activity, he would become aware that he was not thinking positively like them, and felt a non-entity. Indeed he attributes the liking that some of his friends had for him to their feeling that he was not in competition with them. It occurs towards the end of a letter to George begun in October, 1818:

> Think of my Pleasure in Solitude in comparison of my commerce with the world—there I am a child—there they do not know me, not even my most intimate acquaintance—I give in to their feelings as though I were refraining from irritating a little child. Some think me middling, others silly, others foolish—every one thinks he sees my weak side against my will, when in truth it is with my will—I am content to be thought all this because I have in my own breast so great a resource. This is one great reason why they like me so; because they can all show to advantage in a room, and eclipse from a certain tact one who is reckoned to be a good Poet.

Keats' habit of being passively receptive of the unconscious would result in his having a passive receptivity in general. It is not surprising that his attitude of mind in creation should be carried over into his other experience. Translate Endymion's holding two loves in his feeling at once into ideas and you have negative capability, the ability to hold conflicting views in consciousness without feeling obliged to choose one. That this is what he refers to in his letters when he discusses the poet's attitude can be verified by their dates. His letter to Bailey on the poet having no identity was written on November 22, 1817. In a letter with the same date to Reynolds he quotes the passage in *Endymion* that occurs about a hundred lines later than Endymion's statement that he has no identity. There can be no doubt, therefore, that he had the experience he attributes to Endymion in mind when he wrote the letter, since he frequently records in his letters thoughts engendered by poetry written immediately before, the imaginative experience of the poems being clarified in the letters. Here is the passage from the letter:

> I must say one thing that has pressed upon me lately, and increased my Humility and capability of submission—and that is this truth— Men of Genius are great as certain ethereal Chemicals operating on the Mass of neutral intellect—but they have not any individuality, any determined Character.

The statement about 'negative capability' comes later, in a letter

55

dated December 28th, and is not arrived at without further thought. He says there that,

> The excellence of every art is its intensity, capable of making all disagreeables evaporate from their being in close relationship with Beauty and Truth.

Possibly the conflict of opposite feelings and of archetypal terror, if we may call it that, are 'disagreeables'. He goes on to say he has had a dialogue with Dilke during which 'several things dovetailed' in his mind. Then comes his statement:

> at once it struck me what quality went to form a man of achievement, especially in literature, and which Shakespeare possessed so enormously—I mean *Negative Capability*, that is, when a man is capable of being in uncertainties, mysteries, doubts, without any irritable reaching after fact and reason.

It appears that one of the things that 'dovetailed' must have been his own experience of having no identity. Walter Jackson Bate in his life suggests that Hazlitt's *Principles of Human Action*, where he discusses the nature of identity may be another. Indeed this may be a background to the statement in the poem too. But we can be sure that this was the conclusion he himself drew from them. A conclusion that comes from the dovetailing of several things in one's mind is one's own conclusion. This is important considering the attention given by the critics to his theory of negative capability, particularly since during his lectures in the following January and February, which Keats attended, Hazlitt put forward this as characteristic of poets. Precisely what we should conclude I do not know. But we can be sure that Keats had this previous experience of his own, and the resemblance may be a coincidence. Such coincidences are quite common. Moreover if this is indeed a characteristic of poets, it is not surprising that Keats, who explored the workings of his own mind, should have discovered it for himself.

The letter of November 22nd is relevant to *Endymion* in other ways. It is interesting that he should refer to awakening and finding a dream true as significant, since this was what he had just made Endymion do. The letter confirms in general the validity of the sort of analysis of the poem that I have tried to make. He writes:

> O! I wish I was as certain of the end of all your troubles as that of your momentary start about the authenticity of the Imagination. I am certain of nothing but of the holiness of the Heart's affections, and the truth of Imagination. What the Imagination seizes as Beauty must be Truth—whether it existed before or not,—for I

have the same idea of all our passions as of Love: they are all, in their sublime, creative of essential Beauty. In a Word, you may know my favourite speculation by my first Book, and the little Song I sent in my last, which is a representation from the fancy of the probable mode of operating in these Matters. The Imagination may be compared to Adam's dream,—he awoke and found it truth:—I am more zealous in this affair, because I have never yet been able to perceive how anything can be known for truth by consecutive reasoning—and yet it must be. Can it be that even the greatest Philosopher ever arrived at his Goal without putting aside numerous objections? However it may be, O for a life of Sensations rather than of Thoughts! It is 'a Vision in the form of Youth', a shadow of reality to come—and this consideration has further convinced me,— for it has come as auxiliary to another favourite speculation of mine,—that we shall enjoy ourselves hereafter by having what we called happiness on Earth repeated in a finer tone. And yet such a fate can only befall those who delight in Sensation, rather than hunger as you do after Truth. Adam's dream will do here, and seems to be a Conviction that Imagination and its empyreal re-flexion, is the same as human life and its spiritual repetition. But, as I was saying, the simple imaginative Mind may have its rewards in the repetition of its own silent Working coming continually on the Spirit with a fine Suddenness.

— — — — I am continually running away from the subject. Sure this cannot be exactly the case with a complex mind—one that is imaginative, and at the same time careful of its fruits,—who would exist partly on Sensation, partly on thought—to whom it is necessary that 'years should bring the philosophic Mind?' Such a one I con-sider yours, and therefore it is necessary to your eternal happiness that you not only drink this old Wine of Heaven, which I shall call the redigestion of our most ethereal Musings upon Earth, but also increase in knowledge, and know all things.

Since *Endymion* was a work of imagination what it seized on must be truth. Since this cannot be a truth of the exterior world, Keats must have felt he was learning truth of his own interior world by letting his imagination create beauty. His beauties are archetypal images. If the 'little Song' is the Song to Sorrow, which we cannot know for the letter referred to is lost, then it would represent how these matters operate. My view may be prejudiced, but I have shown how it seems to say that sorrow gives values to symbols of the Self, certainly to beauty. His saying that Imagination is a dream that will afterwards be found true is a way of saying what he shows in the poem, that archetypal experience is later verified in external fact. Since this was written about the time he was repeating the dream or archetypal experiences of Books I to III in the waking world of IV it seems a deduction from *Endymion*. He is not just thinking of Endymion waking and finding his dream embraces of the Goddess verified in the arms of The Indian Maid. The dream experiences of the Self in Books II and III are verified in a waking one in Book IV, and the actual feasting of Endymion in the earlier books turns into archetypal feasting in Book IV. In fact, Book IV is a mirroring of Books II and III in reverse. *Endymion* expresses a life of interior Sensations rather than of Thoughts. It is certainly 'a Vision in the form of Youth'; and Keats feels the life of Sensation to be 'a shadow of reality to come'—a point I keep stressing, perhaps *ad nauseam*. He relates this feeling of the dream coming true, to life after death. But it may well be that this intuition really related to his own actual life, since a development in the unconscious, or in what the imagination seizes from the unconscious, is indeed a precursor of a development in consciousness. Jung says it provides the possibility of such a development rather than its necessity. Keats comments that this development can befall only those who delight in this sort of sensation, or intuition, rather than search for truth by thought. That is to say, it is this archetypal activity that will be experienced in another form later. He then says that 'the simple imaginative Mind', which is patently a reference to his own natural way of experiencing, has its reward in the repetition of its own silent workings, that is its unconscious workings, coming continually on the spirit, or into consciousness, with a fine suddenness, as imagination does indeed come into the consciousness of the poet. He therefore concludes that Bailey, the thinker, should drink the wine of Heaven, or archetypal awareness and also know all things. The knowing all things is a seed of thought that was to develop in his mind and appear in *Hyperion*, which he had begun to conceive before he finished *Endymion*, perhaps about this time. This is a difficult passage to understand. If one interprets it as his thoughts about what he had just written in *Endymion* its meaning seems clarified. He ends the letter by saying he has still 500 more lines to write. One need not be literal. But calculating that the book was to be 1,000 words this brings him to just before the Cave of Quietude, which I am approaching in my analysis. The letter illuminates what was to follow in *Endymion*. The Cave of Quietude is celebrated by a feast of all the archetypes in Heaven. The Cave may be an experience of the Imagination and the feast its 'empyreal reflexion'. He says this 'is the same as human life and its spiritual repetition'. This would mean that although he refers the spiritual repetition to a life hereafter, he has a half-awareness that it is in reality something the spirit can experience now in this life—that the deepest inward experiences have archetypal 'reflexions' on a colossal scale; Endymion's deep inward experience in the cave is feasted by the gods and sung through the whole universe.

To return to the poem, the lovers interchange eternal vows as they are carried along

> aloof
> Up in the winds, beneath a starry roof,
> So witless of their doom.

When the moon arises his lady fades 'gaunt and spare In the cold moonshine', and melts in his grasp. How this ought to be understood psychologically is not clear, at least to me. But the mortal lovers were far from the earth, that is far from reality, in their love, carried on the dark steeds of unconsciousness as is common in the first stages of love. It was inevitable that this ecstasy should fade in moonshine. On the other hand if the moon still signifies the Goddess at least of his love, if not indeed the figure of his mother behind it, it could be interpreted as a relapse. I favour the other interpretation, however, since the experience of Endymion's resulting misery leads directly to the Cave of Quietude, the record of a more conscious experience of the Self than those earlier in the poem. We notice, then, that the pattern of Endymion's relationship with the Indian Maid follows that of his relationship with his Goddess. Both include a dream ecstasy, a fall to earth, his love leading to, in the first instance his helping the lovers in the undersea world to oneness, and in the second a daylight experience of it. As Middleton Murry first I think showed, it is obvious that the Cave of Quietude describes what must have been a profound mystical experience of Keats. Since it is crucial in the poem—indeed its climax, I shall quote it at length :

> There lies a den,
> Beyond the seeming confines of the space
> Made for the soul to wander in and trace
> Its own existence, of remotest glooms.
> Dark regions are around it, where the tombs
> Of buried griefs the spirit sees, but scarce
> One hour doth linger weeping, for the pierce
> Of new-born woe it feels more inly smart :
> And in these regions many a venom'd dart
> At random flies; they are the proper home
> Of every ill : the man is yet to come

Who hath not journeyed in this native hell.
But few have ever felt how calm and well
Sleep may be had in that deep den of all.
There anguish does not sting; nor pleasure pall :
Woe-hurricanes beat ever at the gate,
Yet all is still within and desolate.
Beset with plainful gusts, within ye hear
No sound so loud as when on curtain'd bier
The death-watch tick is stifled. Enter none
Who strive therefore : on the sudden it is won.
Just when the sufferer begins to burn,
Then it is free to him; and from an urn,
Still fed by melting ice, he takes a draught—
— — — — — — — — — —
                                        Happy gloom !
Dark Paradise ! where pale becomes the bloom
Of health by due; where silence dreariest
Is most articulate; where hopes infest;
Where those eyes are the brightest far that keep
Their lids shut longest in a dreamless sleep.
O happy spirit-home ! O wondrous soul !
Pregnant with such a den to save the whole
In thine own depth. Hail, gentle Carian !
For never since thy griefs and woes began,
Hast thou felt so content : a grievous feud
Hath led thee to this Cave of Quietude.
Aye, his lull'd soul was there, although upborne
With dangerous speed : and so he did not mourn
Because he knew not whither he was going.
So happy was he, not the aerial blowing
Of trumpets at clear parley from the east
Could rouse from that fine relish, that high feast.

We can learn from this what an experience of the Self is like. The
Cave lies in darkness, in the unconscious. It is surrounded by the
extreme of misery. It is won not by effort but on the sudden. It is a
'Dark Paradise'. It is within the soul, which is 'pregnant with such
a den', and pregnant 'to save the whole' in its 'own depth'. This is
something different from the realization of the Self as an external
palace in the depth of the sea which Endymion entered and perceived. Now it is realized as within his own psyche. He is aware at
once of its being surrounded by the utmost sense of loss, loss of his
intensest ego desire. The 'grievous feud' of being torn almost in
two by conflict has led him there. Jung says all this of the Self.

Endymion illustrates at least three different sorts of awareness of
the Self. The first comes early in Book I where an appreciation of

beauty leads to a sense of oneness, that sense of oneness being an activity of the Self. The second is the imaginative grasp of it as seen in a great many symbolic images in the poem, some of which I have indicated, and preeminently in the union of Venus and Adonis, in the dream of Endymion and his Goddess on Olympus, in the under-sea marriages and in the gathering in the palace of Neptune. It is interesting to consider how far such images communicate to readers a dim awareness of their Self. As a rule when we read such passages we are not aware of the Self, only with luck are deeply moved. How far an imaginative stirring caused by reading imagery of the Self should be called an awareness of it I do not know. But they certainly imply a symbolic experience of the Self in the poet—a dream-like consciousness of it. That of the Cave of Quietude implies a conscious constellation of the Self. It is not presented as a dream image, but as a recollection of a wide awake experience. The two are quite different. The one is imagined, imaged, the other is felt directly not through the medium of images. Keats describes it as a numinous peace of great depth experienced in an environment of misery.

At the end Keats refers to the Cave of Quietude as a 'high feast'. Voices are heard singing,

> Who, who from Dian's feast would be away?

> Who, who away would be
> From Cynthia's wedding and festivity?

Endymion's winning of this goal of life has as its archetypal equivalent the partaking of a eucharistic feast. By passing at once from the Cave of Quietude to Dian's wedding feast Keats implies an eternal, archetypal activity behind the experience of the Self. Endymion has achieved immortality in the Cave of Quietude because he has partaken of what is archetypal and hence eternal. Indeed it may well be that this is the immortality that man really desires and seeks and even tries to prepare himself for rather than a life after the end of existence on earth. Experience of the Self is what gives the sense of being immortal. Again all this is said by Jung.

The song replies to its question, that Hesperus, the star of dawn, that Zephyrus, the west wind, that Flora and that Aquarius would not be away from Dian's wedding. It is interesting that Keats should have selected Aquarius as his first constellation since Jung equates the zone of Aquarius with that where the Self is realized, the zone of the fishes. Keats may have 'thought of' Aquarius in order to include the sea as well as the sky and the earth in rejoicing. He records in the letter already referred to the pleasure that his lines about Aquarius gave him. The 'white shoulders silvery' of the fish are to

> make more bright
> The star-Queen's crescent on her marriage night.

He continues with the other constellations. 'Castor has tamed the planet Lion,' Pollux has mastered the Bear. This may indicate that the wild instincts of man are under control. He asks who is the third? It is the centaur ready to slay some enemy. In Jungian psychology the centaur, half beast, half man is a symbol for man's complete nature. Keats includes Andromeda and all the other constellations. It is possible that Aquarius made the association of ideas that led to the constellations being included. On the other hand Jung takes the constellations to be a projection of his psyche into the sky by primitive man. And it may be that Keats intuited the underlying significance and consequently the relevance of the constellations to the archetypal marriage. The whole archetypal world celebrates when Endymion experiences his Self in the wide-awake consciousness of the Cave of Quietude.

Endymion's horse eventually carries him down to earth.

> His first touch of the earth went nigh to kill.

But he adjusts and relates to the Indian Maid:

> 'Behold upon this happy earth we are;
> Let us aye love each other; —
> — — — — — — — —
>   O destiny!
> Into a labyrinth now my soul would fly,
> But with thy beauty will I deaden it.
> — — — — — — — —
> — — — — —   I have clung
> To nothing, lov'd a nothing, nothing seen
> Or felt but a great dream! O I have been
> Presumptuous against love, against the sky,
> Against all elements, against the tie
> Of mortals each to each, against the blooms
> Of flowers, rush of rivers, and the tombs
> Of heroes gone! Against his proper glory
> Has my own soul conspired: so my story

Will I to children utter, and repent.
There never liv'd a mortal man, who bent
His appetite beyond his natural sphere,
But starv'd and died.'

He says the Indian Maid has 'redeemed' his life

'from too thin breathing : gone and past
Are cloudy phantasms.'

He bids farewell to 'Caverns lone', 'air of visions', 'the monstrous swell
Of visionary seas', and continues,

'No, never more
Shall airy voices cheat me to the shore
Of tangled wonder, breathless and aghast.
Adieu, my daintiest Dream ! although so vast
My love is still for thee. The hour may come
When we shall meet in pure elysium.
On earth I may not love thee; and therefore
Doves will I offer up, and sweetest store
All through the teeming year : so thou wilt shine
On me, and on this damsel fair of mine,
And bless our silver lives.'

Of the Indian Maid he asks 'one human kiss ! One sign of real breath
. . . no more of dreaming'.

Endymion has given up the dream, not to say inflation, of identifying himself with the archetypes, of loving a goddess and of wandering in archetypal regions. He has now arrived at the truth of himself, no longer hob-nobbing with immensities. He sees his former presumption. This is the practical result of the experience of Wholeness in Jungian psychology. Endymion and by implication Keats, is reduced to his real dimension. This is what he has learnt. Experience at the archetypal level reduces everyday experience to its right proportion. And it is, as Endymion finds, adequate, more than adequate since it is everyday experience with a conscious archetypal background. The archetypes still exist, and give significance to wide-awake living. Keats expresses this in two ways. He makes Endymion say he will reunite with his Goddess in Elysium. This is the 'idea' he developed in his letter. Endymion rejects the archetypal experience in favour of exterior reality, but he has a feeling of the interior experiencing as having an eternal validity. So he makes his hero anticipate its coming true in the life after death, which is how he interprets this intuition in his letter. But he knows that the archetypes exist in the present also, and so must be related to. Endymion does this by offering his Goddess a sacrifice and asking her blessing on himself and his love. Their whole life will be lived under her influence as he indicates by calling it 'silver'. That is to say what he rejects is not the undeniable wisdom of archetypal experience but the absurdity of thinking he can make himself immortal and be accepted by a goddess as her lover. So another long stepping of the Imagination to truth has been achieved.

Endymion's interest is now practical; in fact in our terms it is house hunting. 'Now,' he asks, 'Where shall our dwelling be?' He suggests a home in the midst of nature, for his love of her is no less strong. And that must be good psychology—to live in the lap of Mother Nature with a real love. It would not be good psychology to forget the immortals. His Goddess remains as a background but his life is with the real woman; she is his love. He uses his imagination to honour her, but adds,

> 'Still let me live into the joy I seek,—
> For yet the past doth prison me.'

This leads into his statement that he will still be a poet, adding the archetypal image to the exterior experience. A poet is one who is conscious of the archetypal background to life. Moreover Neumann shows that the creative artist never breaks this over-shadowing of the archetypal mother. Keats is still in part her prisoner. Endymion says,

> 'I'll kneel to Vesta, for a flame of fire;
> And to god Phoebus, for a golden lyre;
> To Empress Dian, for a hunting spear;
> To Vesper, for a taper silver-clear,'

and so on, but all will be so that he may love the Indian Maid the better. He says,

> 'Thy mossy footstool shall the altar be
> 'Fore which I'll bend, bending dear love, to thee.'

This is not quite the end of Endymion's story. The Indian Maid says she is 'forbidden' to love him. Then with recollections of Milton's description of Adam and Eve driven from paradise,

> both lovelorn, silent, wan,
> Into the vallies green together went.

The reason the Indian Maid is forbidden is because Endymion is not yet proved.

Here Keats apostrophizes Endymion and tells him he will shortly write of Hyperion. We know that before he finished the poem his interest lapsed, one reason being that he had begun to think of *Hyperion*. It may be that it is about here that this happened. The real story may be complete when Endymion is spiritualized in the Cave of Quietude, the Hymn to Dian sung, and he loves the Indian Maid and seeks a home with her. But Keats had to bring the poem to an artistic conclusion, to bring it full circle and return the hero to the scenes of his birth and to contact with Peona. This completes the design. Perhaps it has a psychological necessity too. Endymion ought not to be left in a wilderness with his love. He must touch the real earth of his home land and make contacts with his relations and friends before his psychological quest is complete. So he wanders back to the stream

> By which he took his first soft poppy dream;

There is Peona. She asks how he can look miserable when he returns with a lady as beautiful as the Indian Maid, for she assumes she has come to wed her brother and be their queen. She tells him that they are all preparing vespers for Cynthia. All their friends are coming. At last Endymion tries some explanation. He says,

> 'Since I saw thee, I have been wide awake
> Night after night, and day by day, until
> Of the empyrean I have drunk my fill.'

Considering how often he has slept and dreamt, this can only mean that he has become aware, that all his dreams have added to his consciousness. He says he will be a hermit that only Peona may visit, when he will tell her wonders. She must take the Indian Maid as her sister. 'That meek unknown' agrees, saying she will be one of Dian's sisterhood. They all three hide their inward misgivings, bending

> Towards common thoughts and things for very fear;

but in reality 'the spirit-blow Was struck, and all were dreamers.' That is, they are all under Dian's influence, which may perhaps indicate dedicated to the Goddess as Keats' muse. Then Endymion calls the two women back and asks them to meet him only once again 'Behind great Dian's temple'. While he waits he prepares himself to die. He thinks how foolish he has been :

> 'Why I have been a butterfly, a lord
> Of flowers, garlands, love-knots, silly posies,

> My kingdom's at its death' — —
> — —   So saying, he
> Tripp'd lightly on, in sort of deathful glee;
> Laughing at the clear stream and setting sun,
> As though they jests had been;

He laughs in bitterness, which soon turns to indignation, for he protests,

> 'I did wed
> Myself to things of light from infancy;
> And thus to be cast out, thus lorn to die,
> Is sure enough to make a mortal man
> Grow impious.'

That he feels bitterness at being let down by the gods shows his integrity of feeling. He hangs on to both sides of his feeling, his respect for the gods and his sense of injustice, as Jung says one ought; the solution to a psychological conflict should not be to give up one side. What was true is true. So Endymion feels that something must be amiss in the siuation. He therefore challenges heaven. He will give the Indian Maid up only if it is heaven's will, and clearly seen to be so. Immediately the dark stranger stands elate, for this is the mood that shows the completion of his spiritualization. She says that he will indeed know.

> And as she spake, into her face there came
> Light, as reflected from a silver flame:

Her black hair turns golden. He beholds 'Phoebe, his passion'. The actual dark stranger, the opposite of his golden Goddess is revealed as the same. He has won his Goddess at last and she him. He kneels down before her 'in a blissful swoon', 'and behold', (at line 1,000) his task completed, 'They vanish'd far away!'

I do not think there is any deep psychological conclusion to be drawn from Endymion disappearing with his Goddess, or the Indian Maid turning into her. If there had been some self-discovery involved, Keats would not have lost interest in the poem and become anxious to get it finished. If he had been free to end it in any other way, we might have expected Endymion to marry the Indian Maid and let his Goddess go. This might have been the right psychology. But Keats had not a choice of ending. The given story he started from was that Endymion should enjoy the love of the Goddess and live for ever with her in utter bliss, not to say asleep on the top of Latmos. The original myth seems to be that of the youth unable to break the dominion of his mother, who keeps him her unconscious thrall. Perhaps Keats started the poem under this thralldom and through writing it stepped by degrees out of that captivity into manhood. His own comments, particularly in his Preface, seem to suggest this. Possibly we should accept the disappearance of Endymion and the moon goddess as signifying the end of this stage in Keats' development, and the ceasing of the goddess to haunt his imagination in this way, although it would not be true to say she never appears in his poetry again.

Although *Endymion* might be best represented left in somewhat of a cloud, I shall try to sum it up clearly on one thread.

Keats set out in Book I to seek the essence of Beauty as the Goddess he dedicated himself to. During the course of it he came to realize that hidden within this search was one that meant more to him, the search for Love. He presents the Goddess as the adored in Book II. During the course of that, he became aware that it was his Self he was seeking. Book III is the story of finding the Self in the archetypal world. Book IV takes him to the final truth that life is not to be lived out in archetypal heroics, but its meaning realized by finding the significance of the archetypal in everyday life. No wonder he said of it, 'My having written that argument will perhaps be of the greatest service to me of anything I ever did.'

CHAPTER TWO

KEATS' development begun in *Endymion* goes on. I shall try first to trace it in his creativeness or his attitude to his muse, and then look in his letters for any carry over into his life.

Keats seemed to become aware when he was writing *Endymion* of layers in his unconscious. Two figures emerge out of an infinite remoteness—the divinity Sleep and Oceanus. Both appear late in the poem.

At the end of the celebration in Neptune's palace, after the hymn to Cupid,

> Was heard no more
> For clamour, when the golden palace door
> Opened again, and from without, in shone
> A new magnificence. On oozy throne
> Smooth-moving came Oceanus the old,
> To take a latest glimpse at his sheep-fold,
> Before he went into his quiet cave
> To muse for ever—

He comes like the surprise when a bass voice held in reserve suddenly enters to give depth to a chorus. And he comes into consciousness only to return for ever into the quiet cave, the ultimate peace of the unconscious. It is as if when Keats achieved manhood, he had an objective view of the ancient deity who had ruled the unconsciousness of his childhood, and watched him disappear for ever. It is almost like the seed of *Hyperion* falling into fertile soil.

Sleep awakes in the fourth book, after Endymion has transmuted his love for his Goddess into that for the mortal woman. They are flying 'High as eagles', Jove's bird, in a flight so giddy that Keats is afraid. 'Muse of my native land,' he cries, 'am I inspir'd?' I suggested that this was the muse of prose reality. With it and only with it he does not

> dread
> Or height, or depth, or width, or any chance
> Precipitous :

and he ends,

> Could I thus sail, and see, and thus await
> Fearless for power of thought, without thine aid?—

He can support this giddy flight because he feels his muse breathing strongly into him (inspiring him). This awareness of a powerful gale from his new muse, so to say, awakens a new consciousness.

> There is a sleepy dusk, an odorous shade
> From some approaching wonder, and behold
> Those winged steeds, with snorting nostrils bold
> Snuff at its faint extreme, and seem to tire,
> Dying to embers from their native fire!
>
> There curl'd a purple mist around them; soon,
> It seem'd as when around the pale new moon
> Sad Zephyr droops the clouds like weeping willow:
> 'Twas Sleep slow journeying with head on pillow.
> For the first time, since he came nigh dead born
> From the old womb of night, his cave forlorn
> Had he left more forlorn; for the first time,
> He felt aloof the day and morning's prime —
> Because into his depth Cimmerian
> There came a dream, showing how a young man,
> Ere a lean bat could plump its wintery skin,
> Would at high Jove's empyreal footstool win
> An immortality, and how espouse
> Jove's daughter, and be reckon'd of his house.
> Now was he slumbering towards heaven's gate,
> That he might at the threshold one hour wait
> To hear the marriage melodies, and then
> Sink downward to his dusky cave again.
> His litter of smooth semilucent mist,
> Diversely ting'd with rose and amethyst,
> Puzzled those eyes that for the centre sought;
> And scarcely for one moment could be caught
> His sluggish form reposing motionless.
> Those two on winged steeds, with all the stress
> Of vision search'd for him, as one would look
> Athwart the sallows of a river nook
> To catch a glance at silver-throated eels, —
> Or from old Skiddaw's top, when fog conceals
> His rugged forehead in a mantle pale,
> With an eye-guess towards some pleasant vale
> Descry a favourite hamlet faint and far.

The sleepy dusk that falls shows a lowering of the threshold of consciousness. Sleep is an indistinct figure seen through mist. He is awakening for the first time. This is emphasized by the repetition of 'For the first time'. And this absolutely new depth of the unconscious, never known before, has awakened from slumber because a young man is about to achieve immortality. Endymion is about to transmute his heavenly marriage on Olympus with a goddess into a wide-awake reality. Sleep overtakes the 'raven horses';

> Upon the spiritless mist have they outspread
> Their ample feathers,

All slumber, and under the god's influence Endymion dreams he 'walks On heaven's pavement', springs towards his Goddess and wakens to behold 'his very dream' turn into the Indian Maid. Then, like Oceanus, Sleep returns to the unconscious again.

By the time he had finished *Endymion*, and through following it out, Keats had become aware of gods from an older or profounder layer of unconsciousness, that then receded into the far background. It is the story of these gods from a deeper layer of the unconscious being superseded that he celebrates in *Hyperion*. He celebrates it with a certain objectivity, not as in *Endymion* pursuing an intuition leading him into the unknown, but looking back on something he has already seen. That is to say *Hyperion* is much nearer allegory than *Endymion*. It begins from a much more aware standpoint, in recollection, stating something already known; in the partnership of unconscious and consciousness the latter guides the pen rather than the former. Consequently it is a much better poem than *Endymion*. On the other hand it can have taught Keats much less about himself, and since what the intuitive reads in his unconscious seems his most genuine experience, this may partly account for why he came to devalue it, and think it rather false. In it he creates a wonderful impression of Titanic powers with lost vitality in a mood of despair. The story was to relate the triumph of beauty over the old gods of power. This shows that his new consciousness involved a completely new sense of values. Our civilization is based on power. The Christian God, like all the other old gods, is a God of might, and western civilization is based on the valuing of power above everything else. What Keats sees is that this is outmoded. The new value is that of beauty. Since we have developed an inhibition against using the word 'beauty', so that it has become meaningless, I shall have to examine Keats' meaning, but here it may be enough to say that it means imagery from the senses felt to have a numinous quality involving great depth of feeling. Put simply, in *Hyperion* Keats narrates a mythological story rather than uses mythological items as an aid to a journey into the unconscious. His imagery carries a numinous quality but the story itself does not. As I see it the myth could not carry what Keats wanted to say; he was bound to find it unsatisfactory. It has some suggestive features, however.

Oceanus is an interesting figure in *Hyperion*. Saturn has lost his majesty, although he is not less than supreme god ruined; he makes a wonderful deposed father-figure. But Oceanus retains his ancient wisdom. Saturn, old god of the heavens and therefore of clear day-light consciousness does not understand what has happened to him, or why. But Oceanus, the old father of the unconscious, undersea world, has lost none of his wisdom. It is equal to the hour. This accords with Jung's view that the wisdom of the unconscious is in-exhaustible in a way that conscious sagacity is not. There are defined limits to consciousness, but none to the unconscious. Saturn is Keats' old consciousness. His dethronement occurred at the place where Keats came to realize that he had no identity. Saturn cries,

> 'I am gone
> Away from my own bosom: I have left
> My strong identity, my real self,'

His agonized call,

> 'Thea! Thea! Thea! where is Saturn?'

reminds us of the cry of woe when the old Endymion disappeared at the dethroning of his Goddess in favour of the Indian Maid. '*Woe to that Endymion! Where is he?*' it asked. Saturn's next question, when he can find words again is,

> 'But cannot I create?
> Cannot I form? Cannot I fashion forth
> Another world, another universe,
> To overbear and crumble this to naught?
> Where is another chaos? Where?'

Keats knows that the answer is that the old god cannot, for he has discovered a new creator, the one that awakened old Sleep from his unconscious.

Hyperion rather than Saturn interests Keats since he is the god poet. He is presented objectively as one already known just as Saturn is, but as one whose wisdom is 'long since fled'. His approaching fall, and Keats' summoning of Apollo, brings into consciousness Cœlus, the father of the even older generation of gods than Saturn's. Just as Oceanus entered the undersea palace of *Endymion* before the new birth, so now before the next new creation a voice from a more remote depth of unconsciousness speaks, a 'region-whisper'. He comes

71

because he knows that his sons must resign their power. Such a disturbance in the archetypal realm awakens a sleeper from the deepest unconscious and he comes with a profounder understanding than his children.

At the council of the fallen gods Oceanus interprets their situation to his contemporaries. He arises now 'with locks not oozy' because he is no longer half-buried as he was in *Endymion*. All his wisdom has been learned. That is to say as a symbol he is dead, for symbolic images have power and remain alive only when half-buried in unconsciousness. They are the means of revealing the half-buried. Once that wisdom has come into clear daylight and nothing of it remains unconscious they no longer have any power and are not living symbols. This is what has happened for most people today with Christian symbols; only lacking Keats' creativeness we tend to remain in a conscious state with nothing to take us into a further knowledge of the unconscious. Keats on the contrary finds symbols from a deeper prior unconsciousness to take their place. The classical gods come from an older hierarchy to bring him a more remote awareness. It is the truth of a further depth that the Oceanus and Sleep of *Endymion*, and Cœlus reveal. And all appear at the climax of new awareness. When Keats' unconscious is shaken to its foundation at the birth of a new dominion, it produces a powerful archetype from the previous rulers. All three come to witness the event. That is to say they represent the birth of a consciousness from a deeper layer able to look at the declining gods objectively as symbols whose meaning is fully perceived and therefore as deposed symbols. We saw that the last book of *Endymion* represents a state of the hero's consciousness when the Indian Maid becomes more real than the Goddess. This does not mean a rejection of the archetypal, of dream symbolism, but that the old symbols have finished their contribution to consciousness. The Indian Maid means what she does to Endymion because she is his goddess made conscious. He dreamt of the goddess and awoke to find that the significance in her was in the Indian Maid, and therefore he rejects the old symbol in her favour. An anomaly may be noticed here. The old gods in *Hyperion* go because a new generation comes to take their place, but the new awareness that deposes them is symbolized by the appearance from the unconscious of a god from an even older generation. Neptune gone, Oceanus comes to the fore, that generation gone, Cœlus. This is what I meant by saying that the myth of *Hyperion* was unsuitable to say what Keats wanted to. The second version of it opens by his coming to Saturn's altar to find his new wisdom. He got no further with it, for what the story indicated was the deposition of Saturn, and yet it is Saturn representing the death of the old life that held the key to Keats' own rebirth. He sacrifices himself to Saturn as holding the solution to life; to write of his deposition would falsify Keats' experience. What lay deeper in his unconscious waiting to be revealed was buried deeper than Saturn; it concerned the older gods yet, not the new generation which he had already clarified.

Let us look, however, at what Keats was able to say in *Hyperion*. There is no ambiguity in his meaning, for it is already fully conscious. Oceanus explains the situation by saying that they 'fall by course of Nature's law', that just as they were not first born, but rose to power when 'The ripe hour came, And with it light', so

> 'Now comes the pain of truth, to whom 'tis pain;
> O folly ! for to bear all naked truths,
> And to envisage circumstance, all calm,
> That is the top of sovereignty.'

Now, he says, 'a fresh perfection treads' on their heels, one more beautiful. Then he adds,

> 'Say, doth the dull soil
> Quarrel with the proud forests it hath fed,
> And feedeth still, more comely than itself?'

Jung points out that the ancient wisdom of the unconscious still feeds the consciousness that has sprung out of it to supersede it. Keats was very well aware of it.

Close on Oceanus' clarification of the situation Apollo, the new god of poetry, is introduced. He is introduced *via* a feminine figure. She weeps for the lost glory, for she has felt the new charm. It is as if she were the muse of the last dispensation converted first, as she must be, for she must resign her hold on poetry if a new poet is to come. She relates how as she sang her tale of sorrow,

> 'There came enchantment with the shifting wind,'

She threw the shell, on which she was accustomed to blow melodies, away,

> 'And a wave fill'd it, as my sense was fill'd
> With that new blissful golden melody.
> A living death was in each gush of sounds,
> Each family of rapturous hurried notes,
> That fell, one after one, yet all at once,
> Like pearl beads dropping sudden from their string :'

Then came 'like a dove leaving its olive perch', a winged music that made her 'sick Of joy and grief at once. Grief overcame'. Then followed a voice

> 'sweeter than all tune,
> And still it cried, "Apollo! young Apollo!
> The morning-bright Apollo! young Apollo!"'

The sea of huge Enceladus with 'overwhelming voice' swallowed hers in wrath, counselling war. Her useless shell filled by the sea may show that Enceladus overwhelmed her in unconsciousness; she will never again inspire any poet.

Keats leaves the old gods and sings of Apollo, the father of all verse. This represents an advance in attitude. It is no longer the archetypal mother, the moon goddess, who inspires him, but the father of all verse. Apollo has left his mother and his twin sister. Keats, we might say, has left his Goddess and Peona. This is no longer a song in moonlight, the twilight consciousness. We may remember that Endymion set off into the underworld of twilight. Now

> The nightingale had ceas'd, and a few stars
> Were lingering in the heavens, while the thrush
> Began calm-throated.

It is the moment of dawn. Apollo, however, and necessarily, has his muse. To him

> With solemn step an awful Goddess came,
> And there was purport in her looks for him,
> Which he with eager guess began to read
> Perplex'd.

The muse of poetry is no longer the bright moon Goddess who has fallen passionately in love with the poet, and who awakens an answering passion in him. In his maturity Keats has a different attitude to his muse. She seeks him with solemn step; she inspires awe in him. She holds meaning which he cannot yet read, an inscrutable story. Moreover she comes with an awful purpose, not winning him to work in passionate love, but asking something terrifying and unsweetened.

Apollo questions her:

> 'How cam'st thou over the unfooted sea?
> Or hath that antique mien and robed form
> Mov'd in these vales invisible till now?
> Sure I have heard those vestments sweeping o'er

74

The fallen leaves, when I have sat alone
In cool mid-forest.

— — — — —

Goddess ! I have beheld those eyes before,
And their eternal calm, and all that face,
Or I have dream'd.'

We can see that she has the characteristics of every muse, and is like
the muse of *Endymion* in this; the poet had intimations of her long
before she came into consciousness; he has long known her, but now
she becomes visible. Apollo (and we must feel Keats also) recognizes
her as belonging to his deepest unconscious; she has an 'antique mien'.
He has seen her eyes before with their 'eternal calm', or has he
dreamed?

>   'Yes,' said the supreme shape,
> Thou hast dream'd of me; and awaking up
> Didst find a lyre all golden by thy side,
> Whose strings touch'd by thy fingers, all the vast
> Unwearied ear of the whole universe
> Listen'd in pain and pleasure at the birth
> Of such new tuneful wonder. Is't not strange
> That thou shouldst weep, so gifted? —
>
> — — — explain thy griefs
> To one who in this lonely isle hath been
> The watcher of thy sleep and hours of life,
> From the young day when first thy infant hand
> Pluck'd witless the weak flowers, till thine arm
> Could bend that bow heroic to all times.
> Show thy heart's secret to an ancient Power
> Who hath forsaken old and sacred thrones
> For prohecies of thee, and for the sake
> Of loveliness new born.'

Apollo then begins the agony that precedes his awakening, and asks
only to have what he must say made clear:

>   'For me, dark, dark,
> And painful vile oblivion seals my eyes:
> I strive to search wherefore I am so sad,
> Until a melancholy numbs my limbs:
>
> — — — — — —
>
> Goddess benign, point forth some unknown thing:
> Are there not other regions than this isle?
>
> — — — — — —
>
> I have heard the cloudy thunder: Where is power?
> Whose hand, whose essense, what divinity
> Makes this alarum in the elements,

While I here idle listen on the shores
In fearless yet in aching ignorance?'

The last line suggests a wider reference. The muse remains silent for Apollo is not yet 'spiritualized' to use the term from the end of *Endymion*. But he can read

'A wondrous less in [her] silent face.'

And that lesson is one neither of beauty, nor of love.

'Knowledge enormous makes a God of me.
Names, deeds, grey legends, dire events, rebellions,
Majesties, sovran voices, agonies,
Creations and destroyings, all at once
Pour into the wide hollows of my brain,
And deify me, as if some blithe wine
Or bright elixir peerless I had drunk,
And so become immortal.'

To understand this we must know what Keats means by knowledge. He seems about this time to be concerned about his own ignorance, and the need for knowledge. I have already noted that in his letter of November 22nd he said that Bailey should have what I called archetypal wisdom and *also* know everything. We cannot date his writing of *Hyperion* precisely, but there is a group of letters that may reflect his thinking on this matter. On Friday, January 23, 1818, when still copying *Endymion* he says:

I think a little change has taken place in my intellect lately—I cannot bear to be uninterested or unemployed, I, who for so long a time have been addicted to passiveness. Nothing is finer for the purposes of great productions than a very gradual ripening of the intellectual powers.

He tells Taylor in a letter in April, probably of the 24th, that he proposes 'to travel over the North this summer'. He says he means 'to follow Solomon's directions, "Get learning—get understanding",' and he continues:

I find earlier days are gone by—I find that I can have no enjoyment in the world but continual drinking of knowledge. I find there is no worthy pursuit but the idea of doing some good to the world. Some do it with their society—some . . . there is but one way for me. The road lies through application, study, and thought. I will pursue it; and for that end purpose retiring for some years. I have been hovering for some time between an exquisite sense of the luxurious, and a love for philosophy.

To Reynolds on May 3rd he writes:

> Were I to study Physic or rather Medicine again, I feel it would not make the least difference in my Poetry; when the mind is in its infancy a Bias is in reality a Bias, but when we have acquired more strength, a Bias becomes no Bias. Every department of Knowledge we see excellent and calculated towards a great whole—I am so convinced of this that I am glad at not having given away my medical Books, which I shall again look over to keep alive the little I know thitherwards; and moreover intend through you and Rice to become a sort of pip-civilian. An extensive knowledge is needful to thinking people—it takes away the heat and fever; and helps, by widening speculation, to ease the Burden of the Mystery, a thing which I begin to understand a little, and which weighed upon you in the most gloomy and true sentence in your letter. The difference of high Sensations with and without knowledge appears to me this: in the latter case we are falling continually ten thousand fathoms deep and being blown up again, without wings, and with all [the] horror of a bare-shouldered creature—in the former case, our shoulders are fledged, and we go through the same air and space without fear.

We should put against this a statement in a letter of February 19, 1818, when he says:

> Memory should not be called Knowledge. Many have original minds who do not think it—they are led away by Custom. Now it appears to me that almost any Man may like the spider spin from his own inwards his own airy Citadel—the points of leaves and twigs on which the spider begins her work are few, and she fills the air with a beautiful circuiting. Man should be content with as few points to tip with the fine Web of his Soul, and weave a tapestry empyrean full of symbols for his spiritual eye, of softness for his spiritual touch, of space for his wandering, of distinctness for his luxury.

In *Endymion* Keats had high sensations, but to make a poet according to *Hyperion*, knowledge also is needed. Keats never defines 'knowledge', as the thinking man would think he ought to. But it certainly includes more than what is commonly so called. It includes the inner effect that knowledge has on the mind, something that prevents it continually falling and being blown high again by the unsteady progress seen for instance in parts of *Endymion*. It includes being able to 'go through the same air and space without fear'. What enables one to do this is consciousness, knowledge of one's own inner workings. But also knowledge of external deeds and majesties and agonies and creations and destructions increase one's awareness in general. They too contribute to wisdom, which comes from experience as well as from consciousness. This sort of comprehensive knowledge is what Apollo reads in that silent face. Her face is silent although meaningful with all meaning because she needs the poet's voice to deliver her wisdom. Apollo with 'enkindled eyes' keeps a steadfast glance 'Trembling with light upon Mnemosyne'. Then comes the death of the old ignorance.

> Soon wild commotions shook him, and made flush
> All the immortal fairness of his limbs;
> Most like the struggle at the gate of death;
> Or liker still to one who should take leave
> Of pale immortal death, and with a pang
> As hot as death's is chill, with fierce convulse
> Die into life : so young Apollo anguish'd :
> His very hair, his golden tresses famed
> Kept undulation round his eager neck.
> During the pain Mnemosyne upheld
> Her arms as one who prophesied.—At length
> Apollo shriek'd;—and lo ! from all his limbs
> Celestial Glory dawn'd : he was a god !

This is more than knowing with the intelligence; it is knowledge felt upon the pulse, with 'intensity', which is what Keats means by experiencing as a poet. He is thinking chiefly of the agony involved in the destruction of present attitudes with their certainties, that necessarily precedes the birth of a new attitude with its new sureness. We can see from a letter written about the time he was writing *Hyperion* in the last months of 1818 that he was going through a period of changing values. He refers to his changing taste in poetry. Of Mrs Tighe and Beattie he says they 'once delighted me—now I see through them and can find nothing in them or weakness. . . . Perhaps a superior being may look upon Shakespeare in the same light— is it possible?' He has, he continues, the same experience in his attitude to women. Then he ends, 'I never can feel certain of any truth, but from a clear perception of its Beauty'. His association seems to be beautiful things for he continues by writing of Guido, Raphael and a book of prints from the church of Milan. But we need some definition of what he meant by beauty. I cannot feel that this has yet been done entirely satisfactorily, yet we cannot understand Keats at all without it. Possibly this is the best place to discuss its meaning.

To understand what Keats meant by beauty we need to discover what his experience of it was like. Before we began to realize how 'inward' was his life, how much he lived by imaginative vision, he was thought to be adequately described as a sensuous poet, a poet who received his chief delight through his senses. That remains true. His poetry is lit up by every sense so obviously that I need not illustrate. But to understand how he experienced we must relate this to his spirituality. Here again it can best be done in terms of Jung's psychology. It is not that Keats' sense awareness is linked with sensuality. We have no real evidence at all that he was sensual, although some critics have tried to prove it. The evidence for his mother being over-sexed is very inconclusive. Keats' early attitude to women erred rather on the side of distance and over-respect; he thought a beautiful woman a goddess. His first letters to young women show a nervous facetiousness. He worked through the sex-feeling in *Endymion* until the hero was spiritualized, and having done so he looked back on his attitude as immature; by the time he wrote *Hyperion* this was in his past. His mature love of Fanny Brawne on his own statement was based first of all on love of her beauty. So much did she feel this that she protested with feminine wisdom and needs that it was an inadequate foundation. Certainly his love for her and possibly his relations with other women had its sex aspect. But if a puritan age had not viewed the sensuous quality of his poetry very doubtfully, no one would have looked for sensuality in him. Although he occasionally refers to sex in his letters and although he may sometime have 'goatish' feelings, a spiritual search absorbed him. No doubt also, his spirituality must have involved its opposite, sensuality. But this is not to say that he was sensual.

If we try to put Keats into one of the Jungian types, we can say that he was introverted rather than extraverted. A young extravert is not absorbed by an inward journey such as that of *Endymion*. From his letters it is clear that he does not understand the thinking type, for he does not know how truth can be arrived at by thinking. It is equally clear that he feels rather than thinks. So obvious is this that it needs no special illustration. Equally clearly he is intuitive. He thinks first of all in images. Even letters clarifying his intuitions are difficult to understand since he uses not concepts but images to convey his meaning, and critics do not all translate them into the same concepts. Indeed some of his 'thinking' is difficult to put into concepts, perhaps none more so than his 'thoughts' about beauty. It is not just that there is a difficult statement in the *Ode on a Grecian Urn*. We find the same identification or coupling of beauty and truth in many of his letters. The word 'beauty' itself is difficult to conceptualize, perhaps impossible. And at no time does he develop logical thought. His 'thinking' remains intuitive to the end. That is to say he images his 'thought' rather than conceptualizes it. All this shows that of the four modes of experiencing differentiated by Jung—thinking, feeling, intuition and sensation, he is possibly partly a feeling type, but first of all intuitive, and consequently his 'inferior function' to use Jung's term is his sensation function.

This needs some explanation. We have become familiar with the idea that we each live in our own private world. Even our physical equipment mediates the external world differently to us. Not only so, perception is now thought to be determined as much by what we expect or look for as by how vibrations causing sounds and sights are mediated to the mind by our nervous organization. That is to say our psychological make-up has a large say in how we perceive our external universe. The intuitive and the sensation types of human being see, feel, taste, hear and smell differently. The man of sensation sees, feels, tastes, hears and smells common facts. The intuitive does not. The intuitive is not much interested in facts. They tend to bore him. They bore him because they feel deficient in reality. This must be even more marked in a poet who is intuitive. Keats' letters occasionally purvey gossip, but rather because he feels that his reader will be interested than because he is so himself. What he seems most interested in are those impressions from his inner world he has lately observed—his periods of lack of feeling, the impression women make on him, his cogitations about pain, about beauty, about how poets differ from other men, and so on. Even his interest in politics lacks detail, details of fact. Why then this excitement over sense impressions?

When Jung talks of the inferior function he means it is inferior in consciousness. The intuitive perceives his world by means of intuitions, rather than by observation of facts. He jumps to conclusions; he perceives the trend of things, their implications. But what is weak in consciousness, exists strongly in the unconscious. Now the unconscious is an undifferentiated chaos. Things before they arrive at consciousness are indistinguishable from each other. We have seen how at the beginning of *Endymion* Keats' love of the goddess of beauty, his muse, was entangled with his youthful ideal love. In a similar way the sense impressions of the intuitive tend to be entangled with unconscious elements that lend them the numinous, mysterious, poetic quality of what is half unconscious. Thus what to the man of sensation is merely unemotionally-toned facts tends to be perceived by the intuitive with an aura of significance. A car horn heard suddenly in distant traffic can give the intuitive an unforgetable impression, a sense of mystery like a voice out of nowhere. A filmy cloud landing on a mountain top out of an otherwise blue sky can appear as if it condensed out of a strange world to deposit a miracle. Such sense impressions appear toned with material from the unconscious. They therefore tend to bear spiritual meanings. It is clear that this happened to Keats and that is why his senses stirred his imagination. In the sonnet written to his brothers for Tom's birthday we see how an object as common as a car horn fishes up a concomitant from the unconscious:

> Small, busy flames play through the fresh laid coals,
> And their faint cracklings o'er our silence creep
> Like whispers of the household gods that keep
> A gentle empire o'er fraternal souls.

Or again he says that the sound of grasshopper and cricket are 'The poetry of earth', the one in summer, and the other in winter. This is most relevant to what Keats means by Beauty. It explains why for him Beauty is the supreme quality, and likewise why it gives his canon of value. His truth was an inner truth, and his doorway into it was through beauty.

It is easy to illustrate how Keats' sense imagery is 'contaminated', to use Jung's word, by accretions from the unconscious. 'Contaminated' in this sense is not a pejorative word. Keats' sense impressions are not pure; unconscious contaminations give them a poetic quality. Margaret Sherwood, in *Undercurrents of Influence in English Romantic Poetry*, noted that he has 'a sense of organic relationship' with nature. That is as much as to say that he projected a great deal of his unconscious onto it. He identified himself with plants and flowers. She attributes his mythological presentation of nature to this. Keats very often has a sense of some human figure in things. This characterizes both his early and his later work. Thus in the early *Epistle to Mathew* each sort of light has its figure—'flush'd Aurora' in roseate dawn, 'white Naiad in a rippling stream', 'rapt seraph in a moonlight beam', and the grass is swept by 'fairy feet'. In the ode *To Autumn* the season is haunted by a mythological being 'sitting careless on a granary floor', or with 'hair soft-lifted by the winnowing wind' or asleep 'on a half-reap'd furrow', or watching 'the last oozings' of the 'cyder-press'. I find myself wanting to say of Autumn that *she* is the 'Close bosom-friend of the maturing sun'— that the human figure is feminine. Perhaps 'bosom-friend' gives this impression. A woman's hair is lifted by the wind rather than a man's.

On the other hand men did the reaping. But the truth may be that Keats did not differentiate his mythological being, that it is neither feminine nor masculine. At all events autumn is a sensation in a mist of imagination. So also the Grecian Urn is the 'still unravish'd bride of quietness', the 'foster-child of silence and slow time'. This is to say that what the physical object meant to Keats was something clouded over by unconscious accretions. He sums up his impression of the urn as a 'silent form' that teases 'us out of thought As doth eternity'. Thus the urn is more than half-buried in an unconscious background. Keats, even when he does not actually personify, thinks of physical objects as having some personal quality. He refers in *Endymion* to 'daffodils With the green world they live in', to clear rills 'That for themselves a cooling covert made 'Gainst the hot season'. He says that 'daisies, vermeil rimm'd and white Hide in deep herbage', that 'Through clouds of fleecy white, laughs the cœrulean sky'. His attitude appears all the more engrained when not expressed as a personification as in,

Let Autumn bold,
With universal tinge of sober gold,
Be all about me when I make an end.

This contamination of his sense impressions by unconscious elements accounts for many characteristics of Keats' style. It likewise accounts for much unsympathetic criticism of details by those without such contaminations. Thus it has been objected to 'globed peonies', which many readers accept with delight, that peonies are not 'globed', made into globes, or even like globes. To anyone who can accept the phrase, Keats seems to be selecting that stage in their growth when the flowers are roughly ball-shaped. Keats does not say 'balled peonies', however, and this would not give delight. Balls are familiar things pitched or kicked about. Globes are rounds of mystery, of fold within fold of significance. But the poetic aspect of such imagery lies in its holding unconscious suggestions impossible to disentangle. Or again in 'The silver, snarling trumpets 'gan to chide' Keats recreates an impression of the timbre of trumpet sound. Possibly he does so chiefly by onomatopoeia. But if we look only at the imagery, we must agree that trumpets neither snarl nor chide. If we try to discover what these words contribute by elaborating their meaning we cannot see how they are at all suitable. Yet for some irreducible reason they make the effect. This unanalysable quality, the impossibility of differentiating them into particles of meaning shows that their significance comes from the unconscious. And this quality characterizes nearly all his sense imagery.

W. J. Bate noted what he called Keats' 'confusion of the senses', which is as much as to say their undifferentiated quality. He instances among others, 'scarlet pain', 'incense-pillowed'. He notes what he calls 'concentration of energy within a static picture', and gives as an example that wonderful line,

> Tall oaks, branch-charmed by the earnest stars.

This is so impregnated with intuitive light that it is not the adjectives from vision that strike us. Here are three concrete objects, tall oaks, branches and stars. It is 'charmed' and 'earnest' that are particularly Keatsian, and it is their imaginative 'contamination' that holds the poetry. But this is not all, for it is impossible for our analytic consciousness to say how far 'branch-charmed' is visual. The addition of 'charmed' adds in some mysterious way (and therefore by unconscious means) to our visual impression. It forces us to sense the stillness of the branches and become aware of the wide area they bless. And these physical qualities in turn add to the sense of charmedness. We could analyse the impression of 'earnest stars' in a similar way. 'Earnest' makes us see or remember the intensity of a star, but if we have that vision, it again gives significance to 'earnestness'.

Keats was well aware of the nature of his sense impressions. He explains his attitude in a sonnet on *The Poet* which Amy Lowell first printed in her life of him. He says of the poet :

> To his sight
> The hush of natural objects opens quite
> To the core : and every secret essence there
> Reveals the elements of good and fair;
> Making him see, where Learning hath no light.

The 'secret essence' is a significance in the unconscious, something connected with the natural object, but not it. This can mean only what it is in the inward experience of the poet. The essential quality of a thing to an introverted intuitive is what it is in his inward experience, which he feels to be more real than the fact of it. Seeing 'where Learning has no light' obviously refers to a mode of realization that does not come from outward experience. It could be paraphrased : seeing through the eyes of the unconscious. But the beginning of *Endymion* makes Keats' best analysis of the effect of beauty on himself. Here he describes the expansion of meaning that he feels behind details of sense delight. He says the beauties of nature lead one to feel in an organic relationship with the earth, that they are

> An endless fountain of immortal drink,
> Pouring into us from the heaven's brink.

He continues,

> Nor do we merely feel these essences
> For one short hour; no, even as the trees
> That whisper round a temple become soon
> Dear as the temple's self, so does the moon,
> The passion poesy, glories infinite,
> Haunt us till they become a cheering light
> Unto our souls, and bound to us so fast,
> That, whether there be shine, or gloom o'ercast,
> They always must be with us, or we die.

This is far from verbiage; it describes the poet's actual experience. So much of Keats' imagination is projected onto sense experience that it was perhaps most of himself. Of the sound of the word 'Endymion' he says,

> The very music of the name has gone
> Into my being.

This is what happens to the introvert. He takes what impresses him greatly into his being, and holds it there.

Jung says that the inferior function is contaminated not only by elements of the unconscious in this way, but that it is frequently entangled with the Self and thus when first developed often brings the Self into consciousness. Keats describes precisely this experience in *Endymion* when the hero is explaining to Peona what he is seeking. He says that his hopes have 'too rainbow large a scope'. What is felt to have a large scope is often an archetype, and the rainbow makes the bridge from consciousness to the Self. Endymion tries to make his meaning clearer by illustrating from a detail:

> 'Fold
> A rose leaf round thy finger's taperness,
> And soothe thy lips:'

he says. Incidentally we may notice that he says not round 'thy finger', but 'thy finger's taperness', for Keats' mind is not working in a factual way. He suggests putting the leaf to the lips to feel it most sensitively. One could hardly find a more sensuous image. It is easy to guess the Freudian's association. Its association for Keats is 'music's kiss'. He continues,

> 'when the airy stress
> Of music's kiss impregnates the free winds,
> And with a sympathetic touch unbinds
> Æolian magic from their lucid wombs:
> Then old songs waken from enclouded tombs;
> Old ditties sigh above their father's grave;
> Ghosts of melodious prophecyings rave
> Round every spot where trod Apollo's foot;
> Bronze clarions awake, and faintly bruit,
> Where long ago a giant battle was;
> And, from the turf, a lullaby doth pass
> In every place where infant Orpheus slept.
> Feel we these things?—that moment have we stept
> Into a sort of oneness, and our state
> Is like a floating spirit's.'

Feeling a rose leaf with his lips takes Keats through old songs, prophecyings, battle notes, to a lullaby where infant Orpheus slept; that is to say to the infancy of the archetypal figure whose music moved all nature. Feeling with the lips is infantile. But Keats' apprehension of it is not, since he is fully aware, unlike the infant. He recognizes his sensation as an ecstacy of the infant Orpheus; that is to say the sensation takes him to the origin of poetry, realized as something archetypal, or even further than the birth of song on earth, to the birth in the archetype. Jung has shown a connection between the earth and the Great Mother. To have a sense of an organic relationship with the earth is to be aware of being rooted in the Great Mother. To be so in unconsciousness is to be in the state of the infant or of the primitive before consciousness has awakened. But Jung makes the point that when the conscious adult has this sense it is a different sense merely because it is conscious. In that situation the adult has extended his consciousness far into the realm of what is usually unconscious; he has won it for consciousness. Keats penetrates further than the archetype of the poet by means of his rose leaf. He concludes with stepping into a sort of oneness when we become a floating spirit. That is to say he has described how the use of his inferior function, his sensation function, has constellated the Self. It is therefore clear that his senses are a vehicle for taking him to the ultimate mystery, to a state like that of a floating spirit, the very opposite of what the experience of the senses means to one whose main function for perceiving is that of sensation.

Thus Keats attaches value to sense delight because it carries an aura of wonder from the unconscious, and because it may constellate the Self. 'Constellate' was a good word of Jung's for the bringing of the Self into consciousness. The Self is like a star, not only a star shining in a dark sky, but a guiding star. It is the inner Pole Star that the heavens revolve round. Whether they do this in the external world may not be true. But it is true of the inner universe. *Endymion* is confirmation that Keats' development as a poet led to the goal of the individuation process in himself. The examination of his attitude to his muse necessarily leads to examining his attitude to his Self. We can therefore define what he meant by 'Beauty'. It refers to sense perception or sense imagery contaminated with archetypal accretions, which if pursued to their furthest awareness constellate the Self. This definition has its vague aspect, for emphasis can be laid on either the physical objects, or on the numinous sense that contamination from the unconscious gives, or on the Self. As a definition it may not help the thinker, for it does not define 'beauty' as one irreducible concept, which is what he wants. But I hope it makes clear that Keats' use of the word was neither sentimental nor muddle-headed. He used it in a reputable way. It has an actual reference, and is neither an abstraction, nor a generalization, and hence is not meaningless even on positivist theory. If the word 'beauty' is useless to a thinker this is no matter. The words 'apple' and 'emotion' may be equally valueless to him, and for the same reason, that they refer to actualities and not to ideas.

With 'knowledge' and 'beauty' elucidated if not defined, we can now say that the new gods of *Hyperion* represent beauty, the search for the Self as modern man's goal, and that knowledge, or the wisdom that comes from experience and consciousness is a prerequisite for it. The old gods who represented the worship of power are outmoded. I hope I have shown that Keats realized that this was his theme before he sat down to write, in fact that this was what he learnt from writing *Endymion*. He obviously did not put it in that way to himself, since I have used Jung for elucidation. But it makes part of Jung's psychology that the creative artist is the first man to intuit the new consciousness of mankind. Neumann's work on modern artists has this basis. So that a poet more than a hundred years before Jung should intuit his findings should not surprise us. But although Keats knew what he was after in his own terms, he did not, when he began *Hyperion*, realize all the implications. By the end he came to do so. This is what I shall now try to show.

Various reasons have been suggested for Keats giving up *Hyperion*. There is not absolute agreement over precisely when he did so since the two versions, *Hyperion* and the second version, *The Fall of Hyperion* or *The Vision of Hyperion*, could both be called *Hyperion* for short in his letters. In one dated August 15, 1819, he says he has 'been writing parts of my "Hyperion".' That would mean finishing the first version, if it is it he is referring to, for he began it in 1818. But my guess would be that he gave up his first version by February, 1819. He says in his letter to George dated 24th:

> I have not gone on with Hyperion, for to tell the truth I have not been in great cue for writing lately— I must wait for the spring to rouse me up a little.

He ends the first version of *Hyperion* after Apollo undergoes the death-like agony that dispels 'aching ignorance'. In a letter dated March 19th he quotes his sonnet, *Why did I laugh*, which tells of his own experience of a death-like agony as I shall show in the next chapter, and says it 'was written with no Agony but that of ignorance'. As phrases that appear in both his poems and letters usually originate in the poem, it would seem as if the 'aching ignorance' of the poem came first, and therefore that he ended the first version in February, his August letters referring to the second attempt. However over a month later, on September 22nd in a letter to Reynolds he certainly refers to the first version, for he talks as if Reynolds were already familiar with it. He says,

> I have given up Hyperion—there were too many Miltonic inversions in it—Miltonic verse cannot be written but in an artful, or rather, artist's humour. I wish to give myself up to other sensations. . . . It may be interesting to you to pick out some lines from Hyperion, and put a mark + to the false beauty proceeding from art, and one || to the true voice of feeling. Upon my soul 'twas imagination—I cannot make the distinction—Every now and then there is a Miltonic intonation—But I cannot make the division properly.

The Miltonic inversions as being the easier both to check and to understand have been emphasized by critics, but I am not at all sure that Miltonic verse being written in an artist's humour is not the more interesting. In a long letter to George, in a passage written perhaps on September 21st, he says,

> I have lately stood on my guard against Milton. Life to him would be death to me. Miltonic verse cannot be written, but is the verse of art. I wish to devote myself to another verse alone.

The relevant difference is that between art and feeling, and what Keats means by them. I suggest that artist's writing is the more objective, with the content clear in one's mind beforehand, as *Paradise Lost* must have been clear, and as the first version of *Hyperion* is clear. The poet can then write as an artist, for his content is in consciousness. The fresh material in the second version of *Hyperion* suggests a method of composition more like that of *Endymion*. By 'false beauty' Keats evidently means not proceeding from feeling. If this is so, then he possibly gave up the first version because he felt that it, and particularly his statements about Apollo, were false to his inner feeling. It is likely too that the sort of verse he wanted to write was a symbol-laden verse in contradistinction to artist's verse where the imagery is too clear in consciousness to be alive as symbols, and hence in comparison is felt by the poet to lack feeling-tone.

In a letter to Reynolds of May 3, 1818, Keats makes interesting observations on how consciousness changes that are relevant to *Hyperion*. He refers to Wordsworth's 'Burden of the mystery' and says that his day has now arrived there, but this was not so in Milton's day. He continues,

> Here I must think Wordsworth is deeper than Milton, though I think it has depended more upon the general and gregarious advance of intellect, than individual greatness of Mind.

If we put this in modern, not to say Jungian terms, we should have to substitute 'consciousness' for intellect. There is little evidence that the intellect has developed in a few centuries, though much that an increase of consciousness came with the romantic movement, and that Coleridge and Wordsworth were in the forefront of that development. He continues his letter by noting that in Milton's time,

> Englishmen were just emancipated from a great superstition, and Men had got hold of certain points and resting-places in reasoning which were too newly born to be doubted, and too much opposed by the Mass of Europe not to be thought ethereal and authentically divine — ...   ... The Reformation produced such immediate and great benefits, that Protestantism was considered under the immediate eye of heaven, and its own remaining dogmas and superstitions then, as it were, regenerated, constituted those resting-places and seeming sure points of Reasoning. . . . [Milton therefore] did not think into the human heart as Wordsworth has done. Yet Milton as a Philosopher had sure as great powers as Wordsworth. What is then to be inferred? O many things. It proves there is really a grand march of intellect, it proves that a mighty Providence subdues the

mightiest minds to the service of the time being, whether it be in human Knowledge or Religion.

This, incidentally is the theme of Jung's *Aion*. It is a conclusion arrived at by Keats from a study of his own mind, and of poetry, and is all the more remarkable since it came before Darwin and modern ideas of progress. It is of course the theme of *Hyperion*; and his own developing awareness may well explain his final dissatisfaction with the poem.

Keats end the first version of *Hyperion* in a passage showing the relationship between the poet and his muse, or more particularly how Apollo is made poet. He left off in the middle of a sentence, for what I quoted was Woodhouse's version with the last six words in pencil not in Keats' hand. Keats' writing ended with 'Celestial'. It omitted 'Glory dawn'd; he was a god'. No one has questioned Woodhouse's implied claim that the pencilled words are Keats'. Keats made other attempts, one ending,

> Apollo shriek'd—and lo he was the God !
> And god like

Therefore Woodhouse's ending represented something in Keats' mind. One wonders why he stuck on the sentence, what it was that made him unable to swallow it. The second version begins with the relationship between Keats and his muse. That is, it begins with the theme on which he stuck in his first version. I think we cannot doubt that in some way he identified himself with Apollo, as he did with Endymion. But if he did identify himself with the archetype of a poet, this was to misrepresent the truth. In a letter of May 10, 1817 already quoted he wrote of himself as a creator, and then checked himself, feeling the unsuitability, as if he were comparable with God. Perhaps a similar feeling made him choke on the statement here. The second version has an intimacy and a human quality quite different from that of the first. It reads as a personal experience and is not objective art. Not only is the poet not a God, but the experience has come nearer to him. It is felt on the pulses and therefore with a grimmer agony than that of Apollo's, which was a 'pale immortal death', 'with a pang As hot as death's is chill'. Apollo's was likewise a death with no risk. The death of the poet that Keats describes himself as suffering in the opening passages of the second version was something he very nearly did not make a resurrection from. It was by no means pale, or that of an immortal, and it had the chill of a mortal's death. The whole passage has other elements that belong to the Keats of that time, and are understandable so. They would not be understandable in the present context. It is a grim picture, a sort of poetry that Keats wrote nowhere else. It is certainly a different sort of poetry from that of the first version. It suggests that the prelude to his theme very much concerns his situation, and that he felt his emphasis should be on his own new experience rather than on that of an outgrown god.

Meanwhile it is not irrelevant to turn to the second aspect of Keats' development that I want to discuss before going on to the immediate background to the Ode to a Nightingale. We should expect anyone so aware of himself to have mature attitudes, and this is what we find. We can see it in such occasional psychological observations as,

> an obstinate Prejudice can seldom be produced but from a gordion complication of feelings, which must take time to unravel.

This comes very near the 'complex' that Jung discovered; it is at least a conscious complex. We see his maturity also in his attitude to his friends. When still a youth in the early twenties he made mature relationships with them, and arrived at a wisdom far beyond his years. This is so evident from his letters that it may be superfluous to illustrate. But I shall do so for emphasis. His maturity is seen in his comments on a quarrel between two of them. In a letter to Bailey, written on January 23, 1818 he says:

> Things have happened lately of great perplexity—you must have heard of them—Reynolds and Haydon retorting and recriminating, and parting for ever—the same thing has happened between Haydon and Hunt. It is unfortunate—Men should bear with each other: there lives not the Man who may not be cut up, aye Lashed to pieces on his weakest side. The best of men have but a portion of good in them—a kind of spiritual yeast in their frames, which creates the ferment of existence—by which a Man is propelled to act, and strive, and buffet with Circumstance. The sure way, Bailey, is first to know a Man's faults, and then be passive—if after that he insensibly draws you towards him then you have no power to break the link. Before I felt interested in either Reynolds or Haydon, I was well read in their faults; yet, knowing them, I have been cementing gradually with both. I have an affection for them both, for reasons almost opposite—and to both must I of necessity cling, supported always by the hope that, when a little time, a few years, shall have tried me more fully in their esteem, I may be able to bring them together. The time must come, because they have both hearts: and they will recollect the best parts of each other, when this gust is overblown.—

Keats was twenty-three when he wrote this. What immature people tend to do when their friends quarrel is to 'side' with one of them.

I was told by a woman old enough to have grandchildren that in a law suit 'the judge sided' with her. Keats not only keeps his head, but looks at the quarrel objectively. It is a sign of his maturity that we cannot discover from this letter, although we can from others, which friend he thought was at fault, or if he thought both. He shows his maturity too in the attitudes he describes himself to have. The immature person sees others in terms of black and white. The sure way to friendship, he says, is to see a person's faults. If you are still drawn to them 'then you have no power to break the link'. His recognition too that one's feelings may be one's masters is mature. He realizes that one is drawn to one's friends not by reason, but by some unconscious factor. It is likewise mature that he recognizes the quarrel as a 'gust', and does not give himself the immature pleasure of indulging in an emotional exaggeration.

At this time he had the greatest respect for Bailey. When he was later to be disillusioned, his friendship did not waver. From other letters we see that he tended to overvalue Haydon. He relied on him as the ideal creator, perhaps overrespecting his advice, certainly over-estimating his genius, and sacrificing himself unwisely in order to lend him money he could not really afford. A more experienced man might have realized that Haydon was no hero, but a person eaten-up with self-concern. He was later proved not only much less of a genius than Keats, but also less able than Keats himself to stand the greatest blow a creator in the arts can receive. When at length Keats in desperate need asked repayment of the debt, he did not put himself about to comply. Keats then wrote to George Keats in September, 1819,

> Before this chancery threat had cut off every legitimate supply of cash from me, I had a little at my disposal. Haydon being very much in want, I lent him £30 of it . . .   . . . I applied to him for payment. He could not. That was no wonder; but Goodman Delver, where was the wonder then? Why marry in this: he did not seem to care much about it, and let me go without my money with almost non-chalance, when he ought to have sold his drawings to supply me. I shall perhaps still be acquainted with him, but for friendship, that is at an end.

Keats' reaction was justified. Haydon had not acted as a friend, much less as an honest man, but there is moderation in his statement: 'I shall perhaps still be acquainted with him'. On October 3rd he wrote a friendly letter to Haydon, modest about himself, genuinely flattering as usual to Haydon. He ends it, 'I am my dear Haydon Yours ever John Keats.'

We have seen how consciousness may develop from a seed in the unconscious emerging in dream imagery or imaginative realization and proceeding to a clear prose awareness. This was illustrated by Keats' treatment of his hero's journey in *Endymion*. Endymion contributed to the heavenly marriage of male and female in the bliss of the Self in the undersea world, experienced it in the heavenly dream on Olympus, then brought it into prose reality by falling in love with a real woman. To illustrate Keats' own development in this way is not so easy, but we see hints of it. We have already had examples of his habit of reporting in his letters thought and truths which had lately struck him, the origin of which can very often be traced to poems he had just written. This shows that he clarified as prose statements imaginative experiences realized in poetic forms. Some of these prose statements have not moved far from their imaginative background. Thus their relationship is easy to recognize. The point I want to make is that the experiences first recorded in poetry, then clarified in prose, represent advances from a dream-like to a clear consciousness, and thus they become available as principles influencing his actions. We can see from the letters that they alter his attitude to life in general. They, therefore, are his own equivalent of Endymion coming down to earth and loving a real woman. His imaginative or inner experience would be sterile and valueless if it remained dreams.

A chronological study of Keats' letters and poems to illustrate this development would be interesting. It might be studied as a periodic interaction between his need to devote himself to poetry and to engage in some other activity. Thus in a letter dated April 17, 1817 he says,

> I find I cannot exist without Poetry—without eternal Poetry—half the day will not do—the whole of it—I began with a little, but habit has made me a Leviathan.

and in one dated January 23, 1818, already quoted,

> I think a little change has taken place in my intellect lately—I cannot bear to be uninterested or unemployed, I, who for so long a time have been addicted to passiveness.

The second quotation records a temporary resting place only, for, both because he was a poet and also because he continued to develop, Keats experienced later addictions to passiveness, which he referred to as indolence. This sort of indolence is an almost necessary condition for writing poetry. The active, conscious mind must be at rest to allow creative material to germinate. When, as in our age, activity is forced upon poets, they tend to use material only from their personal unconscious, not powerful archetypal imagery. Yet such passive creative periods, although necessary, cannot last for ever; if they did they would exhaust the poet. Outward-looking interludes necessarily recur, although how far circumstances induced them in Keats would be interesting to know. But a comprehensive study of the interaction between his poetry and his prose might make a book in itself. I shall attempt to follow only one thread—his developing attitude to pain.

The problem of pain, for such it came to be, appears first in his obsession over joy and sorrow, if 'obsession' is not too exaggerated a word. He accepted both as feelings, but he was stimulated to thoughts about pain. Pain, eventually associated with evil as essential elements in life, came to trouble him. First of all we find merely reports of his feeling miserable, or of being in low spirits, and that he often had to endure this. On May 10, 1817 he refers to his 'horrid Morbidity of Temperament', and may put to his credit (for courage is a virtue) the conclusion, 'I never quite despair'. His calling depression morbid may show that he rejects any justification for it. This was written while he was working on *Endymion*. There, as we have seen, he presents buffetings between extreme joy and extreme sorrow, although the writing of the poem brought knowledge or consciousness more mature where his buffetings were less violent. His letters about this time are concerned with such things as poetry, beauty and the nature of poets. By January, 1818, *Endymion* was in the past, and he had experiences to justify his 'morbidity'. Tom had developed consumption, his friends, as we have seen, were quarrelling. On the 13th he wrote,

> I am quite perplexed in a world of doubts and fancies—there is nothing stable in the world; . . . I was speaking of doubts and fancies—I mean there has been a quarrel of a severe nature between Haydon and Reynolds and another ('the Devil rides upon a fiddle stick') between Hunt and Haydon.

He expresses his gratitude for Bailey's 'probity and disinterestedness' and his brother's 'uprightness' and places such uprightness above 'any marks of genius however splendid'. He seems to value it as evidence for still believing in the goodness of life, which he felt must be its nature, with evil and pain as deviations. But the minor evil of friends quarrelling was felt to have an archetypal significance, which gives a hint of its being something fundamental, for it makes him think of the devil. It is a trifle, a fiddle-stick, but the devil rides on it. He felt it strongly, although he did not exaggerate its dimension—an example of how 'knowledge' enabled him to keep a steady balance. In February we find him criticizing one of his idols. The ability to criticize one's idols shows the acceptance of faults in virtue and a maturing awareness. He writes:

> It may be said that we ought to read our contemporaries, that Wordsworth etc, should have their due from us. But, for the sake of a few fine imaginative or domestic passages, are we to be bullied into a certain Philosophy engendered in the whims of an Egotist? Every man has his speculations, but every man does not brood and peacock over them till he makes a false coinage and deceives himself. . . .
> . . . I don't mean to deny Wordsworth's grandeur and Hunt's merit, but I mean to say we need not be teased with grandeur and merit when we can have them uncontaminated and unobtrusive.

The common form of a development of this nature is first to perceive the difficulty in the distance and unrelated to oneself, and gradually to bear the contemplation in less and less distant forms until one realizes the evil in oneself. In February Keats sees the flaws in his friends and idols, and on January 23rd he had written to Bailey,

> One saying of yours I shall never forget . . . you said, 'Why should woman suffer?' Aye, why should she? . . . These things are, and he, who feels how incompetent the most skyey Knight-errantry is to heal this bruised fairness, is like a sensitive leaf on the hot hand of thought.

The attitude he starts from is that of merely accepting: 'these things are'. But the thought of how one must accept this 'bruised fairness is like a sensitive leaf on the hot hand of thought'. The leaf of the sensitive plant writhes on a hot hand. His acceptance was not cold and unfeeling; that would not indicate a sound psychological state. To contemplate it produced an intense image of pain. Incidentally this makes a good example of an introverted intuitive reaction. As an introvert he takes the idea of pain into himself; as an intuitive he reacts in a painful image.

A letter on March 25th records a great stride forward. Significantly it came in a poem. It is no longer a matter of unfair suffering, of a great poet being an egoist, of friends quarrelling over trifles, nor of the devil riding on a fiddle-stick, which is not only remote and archetypal but made comic, that is to say devalued. Here is the relevant passage from the poem.

> O that our dreamings all, of sleep or wake,
> Would all their colours from the sunset take:
> From something of material sublime,
> Rather than shadow our own soul's day-time

In the dark void of night. For in the world
We jostle,—but my flag is not unfurl'd
On the Admiral-staff,—and so philosophize
I dare not yet! Oh, never will the prize,
High reason, and the love of good and ill,
Be my award! Things cannot to the will
Be settled, but they tease us out of thought;
Or is it that imagination brought
Beyond its proper bound, yet still confin'd,
Lost in a sort of Purgatory blind,
Cannot refer to any standard law
Of either earth or heaven? It is a flaw
In happiness, to see beyond our bourn,—
It forces us in summer skies to mourn,
It spoils the singing of the Nightingale.

    Dear Reynolds! I have a mysterious tale,
And cannot speak it: the first page I read
Upon a Lampit rock of green sea-weed
Among the breakers; 'twas a quiet eve,
The rocks were silent, the wide sea did weave
An untumultuous fringe of silver foam
Along the flat brown sand; I was at home
And should have been most happy,—but I saw
Too far into the sea, where every maw
The greater on the less feeds evermore.—
But I saw too distinct into the core
Of an eternal fierce destruction,
And so from happiness I far was gone.
Still am I sick of it, and tho', to-day,
I've gather'd young spring-leaves, and flowers gay
Of periwinkle and wild strawberry,
Still do I that most fierce destruction see,—
The Shark at savage prey,—the Hawk at pounce,—
The gentle Robin, like a Pard or Ounce,
Ravening a worm,—Away, ye horrid moods!
Moods of one's mind! You know I hate them well.
You know I'd sooner be a clapping Bell
To some Kamtschatcan Missionary Church,
Than with these horrid moods be left i' the lurch.

This expresses a realization of an inherent cruelty and evil at the
heart of nature. It has come upon him from the unconscious as a
mood he not only did not choose but cannot get rid of. He is no
philosopher to understand or accept it. He feels as if he would almost
revert to some comforting Christian superstition rather than endure
it. He has come on 'a flaw in happiness'. This seems to mean, as
I have already suggested, a flaw in the essential goodness of the uni-

verse. Since he thinks of the nightingale's song as being spoilt by it, and the nightingale is often a symbol for the Self, it might mean that it threatens the Self, the One. The poem shows a significant advance in his attitude, since he is suffering from a fundamental cruelty seen in all nature, which he had not before allowed himself to notice. But he rejects the experience. He feels he has brought imagination 'Beyond its proper bound'. He is in danger of letting evil into his world. The integrated person, in Jung's sense, not only has to let evil into his world, but to let it into himself. Evil is now on the edge of Keats' world against his will. 'Away, ye horrid moods!' he cries. It is not yet an experience he can digest in prose reality, if I may put it so.

Keats, however, could not withstand the maturing force within him. He makes a wonderful statement of what he could feel himself to be in a letter to Reynolds on April 27th:

> I lay awake last night listening to the Rain, with a sense of being drowned and rotted like a grain of wheat.

—the first condition for growing. On May 3rd he wrote to Reynolds his famous letter comparing 'human life to a large Mansion of many apartments', the first being 'the Infant, or Thoughtless Chamber, in which we remain as long as we do not think. We remain there a long while'. The second is the 'Chamber of Maiden-Thought' into which we 'are at length imperceptibly impelled by the awakening of the thinking principle within us'. At first we are intoxicated and see there 'nothing but pleasant wonders'. He goes on,

> However among the effects this breathing is father of is that tremendous one of sharpening one's vision into the heart and nature of Man—of convincing one's nerves that the world is full of Misery and Heartbreak, Pain, Sickness, and oppression—whereby this Chamber of Maiden Thought becomes gradually darkened, and at the same time, on all sides of it, many doors are set open—but all dark—all leading to dark passages. We see not the balance of good and evil; we are in a mist, we are now in that state, we feel the 'Burden of the Mystery'.

Then follows the passage comparing Milton and Wordsworth already quoted. Pain and evil are now what 'we feel' (translate he feels) in a mist. Perhaps pains he could not wish away like Tom's illness have brought him here. On June 10th he writes to Bailey,

> Were it in my choice, I would reject a Petrarchal coronation—on account of my dying day, and because women have cancers . . . and

now I am never alone without rejoicing that there is such a thing
as death. . . . Life must be undergone.

Suffering with no justification has entered his world and although he
does not make anything of it, he accepts it. That is all for the moment.
I shall pick up the thread again in the next chapter, where it is
relevant.

Meanwhile Keats toured Scotland, came home suffering from the
sore throat that eventually led to his death, nursed Tom, who died
at the end of the year, had anxiety over George in America, and
suffered devastating criticism of *Endymion*. But all was not misery.
He fell in love with Fanny Brawne, and he wrote *The Eve of St. Agnes*,
a romance of sheer happiness. Since it is easy to overstress Keats'
misery, and I may tend to do so, I shall try to right the balance by
saying something about the *Eve* before I proceed.

The Eve of St. Agnes expresses love and light and warmth and life
as a core to hate and chill and death. The lover comes out of the
freezing night, braves danger and hatred, traverses intricate dark
passages with the help of the old nurse and prepares a bridal feast
for his love. He watches her undress in rose-tinted light from the
coloured glass window and wakens her from a dream of love, to
persuade her to flee with him to the southern moors. Whether read
merely for its romance or with awareness of its symbolic depth (for
nearly every detail of its structure I have reported is symbolism for the
approach to the Self) it scintillates courage and happiness.

Not only are the theme and the structure of the story felt to have
more than their obvious significance, every detail of its sensuous
beauty reflects some facet of its total meaning. It opens with chill :

> St. Agnes' Eve—Ah, bitter chill it was !
> The owl, for all his feathers, was a-cold;
> The hare limp'd trembling through the frozen grass,
> And silent was the flock in woolly fold :
> Numb were the Beadsman's fingers, while he told
> His rosary, and while his frosted breath,
> Like pious incense from a censer old,
> Seem'd taking flight for heaven, without a death,
> Past the sweet Virgin's picture, while his prayer he saith.

It ends with a chill even more profound. At the core is Madeline's
warm room with the marriage feast, where she awakes from her dream
of love to the reality of it. It looks as if the poem was written out
of an intensity of love involving Keats' whole self. Love is at the
centre, radiating into every phrase of the poem, and giving it its

quality. Amy Lowell noted this homogenous texture, with the whole felt in the details. It might be an exaggeration to say that no detail could have appeared phrased exactly so in any other poem, but only an exaggeration. Thus when Madeline is described as

> Clasp'd like a missal where swart Paynims pray;

the meaning is in a sense determined by the poem as a whole. She is asleep; so the book is closed. But also, she is like a missal, a holy thing, clasped in black hands, as it is when paynims pray, a thing of light in the blackness, an unopened mystery. Since this is a symbol, its full meaning is impossible to fathom. It could be an image for the situation of the whole poem, a thing of light in a worshipping darkness. The contrast of such opposites is never lost sight of in the poem. Porphyro calls his love his 'silver shrine' and says,

> here will I take my rest
> After so many hours of toil and quest,
> A famish'd pilgrim,—sav'd by miracle.

This the seeker can say at the end of the quest for the Self. In Madeline's room, which is 'this paradise', when Porphyro is entranced and near the climax, he sets the table for the feast.

> Then by the bed-side, where the faded moon
> Made a dim, silver twilight, soft he set
> A table, and, half anguish'd, threw thereon
> A cloth of woven crimson, gold, and jet:—

But the sound of the revelry of his foes bursts in.

> The boisterous, midnight, festive clarion,
> The kettle-drum, and far-heard clarinet,
> Affray his ears, though but in dying tone:—
> The hall door shuts again, and all the noise is gone.

When he learns that she loves him,

> Beyond a mortal man impassion'd far
> At these voluptuous accents, he arose,
> Ethereal, flush'd, and like a throbbing star
> Seen mid the sapphire heaven's deep repose;
> Into her dream he melted, as the rose
> Blendeth its odour with the violet,—
> Solution sweet: meantime the frost-wind blows
> Like Love's alarum pattering the sharp sleet
> Against the window-panes; St. Agnes' moon hath set.

> 'Tis dark: quick pattereth the flaw-blown sleet:

The feeling of the consummation of their marriage is achieved to the din of foemen and the sound of the storm pattering on the window— the colour-charmed window. He recalls her to consciousness of their state,

> 'Arise—arise! the morning is at hand;—
> The bloated wassailers will never heed:—
> Let us away, my love, with happy speed;'
>
> — — —
>
> 'Awake! arise! my love, and fearless be,
> For o'er the southern moors I have a home for thee.'
>
> She hurried at his words, beset with fears,
> For there were sleeping dragons all around,
>
> — — —
>
> They glide, like phantoms, into the wide hall;
> Like phantoms, to the iron porch, they glide;
> Where lay the Porter, in uneasy sprawl,
> With a huge empty flaggon by his side:
> The wakeful bloodhound rose, and shook his hide,
> But his sagacious eye an inmate owns:
> By one, and one, the bolts full easy slide:—
> The chains lie silent on the footworn stones:—
> The key turns, and the door upon its hinges groans.
>
> And they are gone: aye, ages long ago
> These lovers fled away into the storm.
> That night the Baron dreamt of many a woe,
> And all his warrior-guests, with shade and form
> Of witch, and demon, and large coffin-worm,
> Were long be-nightmar'd. Angela the old
> Died palsy-twitch'd, with meagre face deform;
> The Beadsman, after thousand aves told,
> For aye unsought for slept among his ashes cold.

This is romantic love in a world of hate and death. It suggests also the core of the Self in a world of danger, a throbbing star in the dark sky. It is the intensest poetry, and perhaps necessarily therefore, involves a stirring of the sensitive reader to at least a dim awareness of a central core of mystery. It is interesting as showing the Self operating artistically, both giving the poem a satisfying structure and contributing depth of association to the imagery. It is the finest of all Keats' narrative poems, conceived as a whole and with no fresh growths from his unconscious intruding to destroy it, as happened in *Hyperion*, where, as it were, a wild oak sprang up to spoil his planned landscape. Nor has he chosen an old myth, as in *Endymion*,

99

that imposes its fixed and unfitting ending on what was essentially a wild growth with its natural laws of development. It achieves a perfect balance of spontaneous feeling and art.

The poem was followed by a fallow period, one also of depression and idleness, out of which as a culmination comes the *Ode to a Nightingale*, and also a development of his attitude to pain and evil.

CHAPTER THREE

The *Ode to a Nightingale* has verbal echoes both from Keats' own work and from that of others, so many that it would justify a study like Livingston Lowes' of *The Ancient Mariner*. But it is unlikely that my theme would gain much from this study. Verbal echoes make the bricks of poetry. A poet who does not use those from his reading must use others from familiar speech. He, like the architect, does not make the stones with which he builds. These give a certain colour to his poetry, a distinguishing colour, but they no more determine the structure of his poems than the red granite which colours Peterhead makes the structure of its houses differ from those in Aberdeen where granite is grey. We need not devalue the influence of echoes in poetry (or the colour of bricks in architecture) but they do not determine the poet's intention, conscious or unconscious. Echoes lead only bad poets, the empty brain reverberating them. Although no poet could write if he were not sensitive to words, even in love with them, and although Keats uses words with a full awareness of their associations they do not lead him in his mature work. If we concentrate on echoes, and particularly if we concentrate on those from others, they can bemuse us, for it is the structure of the poems that carries the intention, words being placed to catch a significance given by their context. The same words and echoes jumbled would be meaningless. In their new place unconscious borrowings reflect a new light.

I shall take one example showing the danger of following Keats' echoes, in order to justify neglecting them as a background to the *Ode*. Robert Gittings, in *The Living Year*, points out that Keats was reading Burton's *Anatomy of Melancholy* about the time he wrote on the Grecian urn. He argues that Burton provides 'much of the general philosophy' of the ode. Burton, he says, refers to 'Plato to show that Beauty is a good in itself', and develops 'the Platonic theme that Good and Beauty and Wisdom are identical, that virtue is a good and a beauty in itself, and is the only way of expressing an eternal truth:' He quotes from Burton, 'No beauty leaves such an impression, strikes so deep, or links the souls of men closer than virtue.' There are other quotations from Burton to the same effect. But this is to bedevil Keats' meaning, for Burton's and Plato's proposition is not his at all. They say that virtue links goodness and beauty and is the only way to express eternal truths. But Keats has only two terms in his statement. He says 'Beauty is truth, truth beauty', omitting the fusing third, virtue or goodness. Moreover he says that the identity of beauty and truth is *all* we need to know. If Keats' memory of Burton was conscious, then he deliberately excluded goodness and virtue, and if his memory was unconscious this exclusion is no less significant. Moral sentiment makes no part of Keats' poetry. In fact, he disliked didactic art as having 'a palpable design' on us, and his letters show from the early days a recurrent coupling of beauty and truth.

Although I propose to neglect its verbal background except where it is relevant to the meaning, the *Ode to a Nightingale* cannot be understood without the background of Keats' experience of life. Between the writing of *The Eve of St. Agnes*, which is a high water mark and the *Ode to a Nightingale*, his sea ebbed into a great depression to return in the high tide of the great odes. In this chapter I shall investigate that ebb and flow as the immediate background to the *Ode*.

To begin the study we might note Keats' explicit references in the *Ode* to his previous experience. In stanza III he refers to youth that 'grows pale, and spectre-thin, and dies'. This is certainly something that moved him in the death of Tom, whom he nursed through the last stages of consumption and who had died a few months before. It is likely that his experience as a medical student in hospital accounts for men sitting and hearing each other groan, where also, if not elsewhere, he must have seen palsy shake 'a few, sad, last gray hairs'. Whether any particular memory is reflected in Beauty losing 'her lustrous eyes' we cannot be sure, nor whether he himself was the young lover who did not pine 'beyond to-morrow'. But it is very likely. Robert Gittings gives evidence suggesting that Isabella Jones might be the Beauty referred to, and that Keats fell in love with Fanny Brawne before he had broken off his affair with her. If so he may be the young lover. In any case his new love put out his old. Middleton Murry objected to Gittings' surmise but his most strongly-felt argument seems to be that since Keats had an exceptionally fine character, and since to behave like this would be caddish, therefore he should not be accused of it. Although possibly no one understood Keats better than Murry, I cannot feel his argument sound. Love is not a matter of choice. Even on Gittings' showing it looks as if Isabella may have wooed Keats rather than he her, and it is clear that Keats fell in love with Fanny Brawne almost in spite of himself. He began by criticizing her, fell into having tiffs with her, and then into loving her. That is to say it was a developing relationship. And there is no doubt that his love for her was a much deeper involvement than that for Isabella. I should therefore think it likely, although we cannot know what the actual facts were, that his reference to lustrous eyes fading and young lovers being fickle involves self-criticism spoiling the experience of the nightingale's song. If this was self-criticism the pain of it must have been all the deeper. Indeed it needs this interpretation to make the young lover's fickleness heavy enough to weigh among life's miseries with youths dying of consumption and old men groaning away their last days.

Gittings attributes the depression that preceded the Ode to a Nightingale chiefly to a complication over Isabella Jones and Fanny Brawne and to the realization that its bad reviews had ruined the sale of Endymion. This is most likely, although it does not take us far. Keats was subject to depressions for 'inward' reasons. If these external circumstances caused his depression, it must have been because they stirred up a far-reaching inner conflict, which I shall examine.

I left off tracing Keats' development as revealed by his letters written before this period, where the evidence ended. The process of inner development once begun tends to continue, although not necessarily without resting. Circumstances may accelerate or retard it, but it works also by inward compulsions. Consciousness depends on the differentiation of undifferentiated wholes into their constituent opposites. So the process of becoming increasingly aware of one's inward workings, of learning to 'know oneself' is largely a matter of conflicts arising and being resolved. This frequently involves depression, and indeed a depression the cause of which is not at all clear to oneself often precedes it. When the conflict reaches its intensest, if the sufferer is lucky, the opposite factors are resolved into the whole that included them at first in unawareness. Jung talks of 'a third element' that comes into consciousness that was wholly unknown before, in the light of which both sides of the opposites involved are held. A somewhat similar resolution I have already shown in the sonnet, When I have fears. Keats referred there to attaining a state when the fears engendered by his awareness of his puny mortal life were resolved by a realization of archetypal richness. His archetypal potentiality, or his potentiality for greatness, and his merely limited human capacity were then both held in consciousness without conflict, as opposites. There the organizing activity of the Self had obviously been at work.

A similar experience must have preceded the writing of his sonnet, *Why did I laugh,* which ended this period of depression.

> Why did I laugh to-night? No voice will tell:
>   No God, no Demon of severe response,
>   Deigns to reply from heaven or from Hell.
> Then to my human heart I turn at once.
> Heart! Thou and I are here sad and alone;
>   I say, why did I laugh! O mortal pain!
> O Darkness! Darkness! ever must I moan,
>   To question Heaven and Hell and Heart in vain.
> Why did I laugh? I know this Being's lease,
>   My fancy to its utmost blisses spreads;
> Yet would I on this very midnight cease,
>   And the world's gaudy ensigns see in shreds;
> Verse, Fame and Beauty are intense indeed,
> But Death intenser—Death is Life's high meed.

I take it that Keats asks the question because he does not know the answer. He asks it three times. First he asks heaven and Hell, 'Hell' having the capital letter; it concerns something archetypal. He also asks his heart, his feeling. Because of this it has been suggested that the question has something to do with Fanny Brawne, but even if it had, to leave it at that would be superficial. He gives his deduction in the sestet, by commenting that he knows that life (this Being's lease) must end, and although his imagination has spread to its utmost bliss, yet he would choose to die this very midnight and resign all the 'gaudy ensigns' of life and see them in shreds. The gaudy blisses are those of verse, fame and beauty, which concern his intensest life. But death is the intensest experience in life, and moreover death is life's greatest reward. In fact it looks as if this were Heidegger's 'authentic' experience of life, or of life in its authenticity. Keats laughed no doubt because to realize this makes his old attitude to verse, fame and beauty as pillars of his universe, ridiculous. It was a ridiculous, because a sudden reversal of his whole attitude to life, the unexpectedness of which might well make him laugh. He laughs too from relief. If he had been held and driven by these desires and aims, to feel released from them must be to have a burden drop from his shoulders in sudden relaxation. Keats had arrived at a basic paradox. Although death is the end of life's bliss, it is also life's final goal. A statement of Jung's might make the best comment. In *The Structure and Dynamics of the Psyche* he writes:

> Like a projectile flying to its goal, life ends in death. Even its ascent and its zenith are only steps and means to this goal. This paradoxical

formula is no more than a logical deduction from the fact that life strives towards a goal and is determined by an aim.

Keats, of course, came to this conclusion not as a logical deduction but as the feeling termination of his midnight experience. A logical deduction does not make one laugh as the sudden reversal of feeling can.

There is an interesting parallel where Endymion suddenly realizes he has been a lord of silly posies, and thus is justly served by having his dream denied him. He feels a dreadful glee, and laughs as though the setting sun had been a jest. Endymion had suffered just such a reversal of attitude. He laughed at the foolishness he now perceived his old attitude to be. I think it can be shown that this was precisely the experience behind the sonnet, for we can get closer to it by looking at Keats' reflections on the morning after in his journal letter to George:

This morning I am in a sort of temper, indolent and supremely careless . . . . . . my passions are all asleep, from my having slumbered till nearly eleven, and weakened the animal fibre all over me, to a delightful sensation, about three degrees on this side of faintness. . . . . . . In this state of effeminacy the fibres of the brain are relaxed in common with the rest of the body, and to such a happy degree that pleasure has no show of enticement and pain no unbearable power. Neither Poetry, nor Ambition, nor Love have any alertness of countenance as they pass by me; they seem rather like figures on a Greek vase—a Man and two women whom no one but myself could distinguish in their disguisement. This is the only happiness, and is a rare instance of the advantage of the body overpowering the Mind . . . . . . we have leisure to reason on the misfortunes of our friends; our own touch us too nearly for words. Very few men have ever arrived at a complete disinterestedness of Mind: very few have been influenced by a pure desire of the benefit of others,—in the greater part of the Benefactors of Humanity some meretricious motive has sullied their greatness—some melodramatic scenery has fascinated them. From the manner in which I feel Haslam's misfortune I perceive how far I am from any humble standard of disinterestedness. Yet this feeling ought to be carried to its highest pitch, as there is no fear of its ever injuring society— which it would do, I fear, pushed to an extremity. For in wild nature the Hawk would lose his Breakfast of Robins and the Robin his of Worms—the Lion must starve as well as the Swallow. The greater part of Men make their way with the same instinctiveness, the same unwandering eye from their purposes, the same animal eagerness as the Hawk. The Hawk wants a Mate, so does the Man— look at them both, they set about it and procure one in the same manner. They want both a nest and they both set about one in the same manner—they get their food in the same manner. The noble animal Man for his amusement smokes his pipe—the Hawk balances about the clouds—that is the only difference of their leisures. This it is that makes the Amusement of Life—to a speculative Mind—I go among the Fields and catch a glimpse of a Stoat or a fieldmouse peeping out of the withered grass—the creature hath a purpose, and its eyes are bright with it. I go amongst the buildings of a city and I see a man hurrying along—to what? the creature has a purpose and his eyes are bright with it. But then, as Wordsworth says, 'we have all one human heart—' There is an electric fire in human nature tending to purify—so that among these human creatures there is continually some birth of new heroism. The pity is, that we must wonder at it, as we should at finding a pearl in rubbish. I have no doubt that thousands of people never heard of have had hearts completely disinterested: I can remember but two—Socrates and Jesus—Their histories evince it. What I heard a little time ago, Taylor observe with respect to Socrates, may be said of Jesus—That he was so great a man that though he transmitted no writing of his own to posterity, we have his Mind and his sayings and his greatness handed to us by others. It is to be lamented that the history of the latter was written and revised by Men interested in the pious frauds of Religion. Yet through all this I see his splendour. Even here, though I myself am pursuing the same instinctive course as the veriest human animal you can think of, I am, however young, writing at random, straining at particles of light in the midst of a great darkness, without knowing the bearing of any one assertion, of any one opinion. Yet may I not in this be free from sin? May there not be superior beings, amused with any graceful, though instinctive, attitude my mind may fall into as I am entertained with the alertness of the Stoat or the anxiety of a Deer? Though a quarrel in the Streets is a thing to be hated, the energies displayed in it are fine; the commonest Man shows a grace in his quarrel. By a superior Being our reasonings may take the same tone—though erroneous they may be fine. This is the very thing in which consists Poetry, and if so it is not so fine a thing as philosophy—for the same reason that an eagle is not so fine a thing as a truth. Give me this credit—Do you not think I strive—to know myself? Give me this credit, and you will not think that on my account I repeat Milton's lines—

'How charming is divine Philosophy
Not harsh and crabbed, as dull fools suppose
But musical as is Apollo's lute'—

No—no for myself—feeling grateful as I do to have got into a state of mind to relish them properly. Nothing ever becomes real till it is experienced—even a Proverb is no proverb to you till your Life has illustrated it. I am ever afraid that your anxiety for me will lead you to fear for the violence of my temperament continually smothered down: for that reason I did not intend to have sent you

106

the following sonnet—but look over the two last pages and ask your-selves whether I have not that in me which will bear the buffets of the world. It will be the best comment on my sonnet; it will show you that it was written with no Agony but that of ignorance; with no thirst of anything but Knowledge when pushed to the point though the first steps to it were through my human passions—they went away and I wrote with my Mind—and perhaps I must confess a little bit of my heart—

After copying *Why did I laugh*, he ends his writing for the day,

> I went to bed and enjoyed uninterrupted sleep. Sane I went to bed and sane I arose.

We can deduce much from this. If Keats went to bed sane it implied that he was not sane before he wrote the sonnet; he now writes in the relaxed mood after a conflict has been resolved. Although he describes it as a bodily feeling that has invaded his spirit, it is much more likely that his body as well as his mind relaxed when the strain he had endured ended. After all he says he went to bed sane. Presumably this sanity induced both his long refreshing sleep and his morning peace of mind. If neither poetry nor ambition nor love have any alertness of countenance now, this implies that their countenance was too alert before, that these—his obsessions—were the figures in his conflict. Then, as is usual with him, he writes himself down to what was the real trouble at the bottom of his mind, the Hawk breakfasting on Robins and the Robin on worms. The lion as well as the swallow would starve if they did not prey on others. And immediately he says that man has the same animal eagerness as the Hawk. This is the unwelcome truth that overwhelmed him a year ago, and which he suppressed as too agonizing. He now accepts it in peace of mind. The whole mood of his letter is one of undisturbed contemplation, and of what before he felt to be shattering. He now sees that this evil belongs to the nature of the universe. The animal's eyes are bright with a purpose. So is man's. Man differs from the animal only in find-ing a pearl in the rubbish. Keats himself is pursuing the course of his own purposes but 'straining at particles of light in the midst of a great darkness, without knowing the bearing of any one assertion, of any one opinion', for poetry makes part of the instinctive life quite as much as hunting for food or mating. Poetry is not so fine as philo-sophy only as the eagle is not so fine as truth. That is to say, the philosopher is conscious and *knows* what the poet images and feels. This has just been illustrated by putting Jung's comment beside Keats' sonnet. It is illustrated also by reading Keats' letter as comment on his sonnet. This he states modestly, for there is a new modesty in this letter. He says he is trying to be the philosopher, trying to know himself. He has now got into that state of knowing himself as far as this experience goes. What he felt before like an eagle, as a poet knows, he now realizes in a different way with a clear consciousness. He then copies out *Why did I laugh*, and says his observations make the best comment on it, that it was written with no agony but that of ignorance. That is to say his letter is a gloss on the poem. The agony behind the sonnet was an eagle agony, but disappeared with the understanding of it.

However, we can get nearer to the experience than this. The animal's passions, he says, drive it to kill for food and to mate. These do not seem to be the passions that Keats is concerned about, although he says a man in love is as self-absorbed as an animal in the same state. He discusses disinterestedness. Now earlier letters show that he valued disinterestedness as the greatest virtue. He thought Bailey had it in a high degree, and also his sister-in-law, as she proved by facing going to America with George. He wrote of her,

> She is the most disinterested woman I ever knew—that is to say, she goes beyond degree in it. To see an entirely disinterested girl quite happy is the most pleasant and extraordinary thing in the world.

(If he had been a woman, he might have recognized this as being in love.) He found in the end that Bailey had not this virtue in any outstanding way and by now can say that the only completely disinterested people he can think of are Socrates and Jesus. And he relates self-interest with the animal's instincts of killing and mating. It is entirely self-absorbed. This is a new perception. Hitherto he has expected disinterestedness of his friends and noted with implied criticism their failure. What one expects of one's friends one usually imagines oneself to possess. And indeed Keats had this virtue if not in any extraordinary way, certainly in a more than average degree. His letter now implies the opposite. He has discovered that he is not himself disinterested, that he has an animal self-partiality, that he is implacably self-seeking. This seems a new self-knowledge—the discovery that he is ego-centred. He implies that it is this ego-centredness that gives him his purpose in life. His eyes are bright with it. But he has discovered not only this; he goes on to say that a superior being looking on may find some good in it as he sees some good in the stoat's purposes. He has now realized the darkness of this truth of his own fundamental selfishness giving him his purposes, as being of the nature of the universe (and therefore as archetypally-determined) and he has accepted it as inevitable, as having therefore some value. It is fundamental in all nature, and in himself as a part of nature. He thereby accepts death, since he gives complete submission to what man must give submission to if he is to be whole—submission to the nature of the universe with its evil no less than its good, however he may dislike evil. That is he accepts the universe as not made to his pattern, but on a pattern he finds in himself, and which he no longer hides from himself, crying 'away' to. This acceptance of death involves a complete abnegation of the ego, and therefore complete submission to the Self. Moreover he has gone through the whole experience to its absolute finality, to such a clear consciousness of it that he can express it in his letter without fumbling. He could not have been clearer if he had lived a hundred and fifty years later when Jung would have provided him with a new jargon for its expression, as he has provided the means of our understanding it.

Now *Why did I laugh* refers not to disinterestedness but to verse, fame and beauty, and it is poetry, ambition and love that Keats refers to in his letter. This suggests that he discovered his own baseness, his own lack of disinterestedness, his ego-centredness precisely in his attitude to these three things—that he discovered it as the purpose in his love, in his writing of poetry and in his desire for fame. This would involve the realization precisely where he thought his aims purest. It requires little imagination to see what an agonizing experience this must have been. But he says it was an agony of ignorance. His new understanding has taken the sting out of it. Intellectual understanding cannot do this. Only the inner experience of wholeness, the experience of the Self can hold this agony in peace. Wholeness is not grasped by thought, which is only one of man's functions. Thinking lacks feeling; it deals only in ideas, in the form and shape of experience, without its body or content. The intellect can contemplate the utmost horror unshaken. A man of pure thought could have come to Keats' conclusion with a quiet pulse, without any involvement in what he contemplates. But Keats was not this sort of man; he felt involved in all his perceptions. We have seen that his first intimations of the Hawk at prey shook him to his foundations. He states that his sonnet involved an agony. Therefore the resolution of that agony must have involved an experience of greater depth and wholeness. Such a resolution involves the Self, and brings with it a reversal of the old attitudes and a new wisdom, just such a wisdom as he reveals in this letter. And more, the shift from ego consciousness to

Self consciousness brings with it a state when 'pleasure has no show of enticement and pain no unbearable power'. This could be a paraphrase of Jung describing the difference that Self awareness brings to one's experience of living.

It remains to show Keats' reversal in attitude. We cannot follow it up as far as his love was concerned. He was at the beginning of that experience and had other agonies in store. But we can trace it as far as it concerned his poetry and fame. I shall postpone dealing with how it affected his attitude to poetry, and deal with its effect on his attitude to fame. Until now Keats thought no shame to write for fame. Indeed in one of his early poems, his epistle *To my Brother George*, he makes a dying poet console himself by saying that his poems will be in the mouths of brides, that mothers will sing his lullabies, 'The sage will mingle with each moral theme My happy thoughts' and politicians quote him. Keats adds,

> Ah, my dear friend and brother,
> Could I, at once, my mad ambition smother,
> For tasting joys like these, sure I should be
> Happier, and dearer to society.

It is true, however, that fame was never his sole motive, as how could it be, for he adds that

> When some bright thought has darted through my brain :
> Through all that day I've felt a greater pleasure
> Than if I'd brought to light a hidden treasure.

In another early poem, *Sleep and Poetry*, he lists as one of the poet's joys,

> To see the laurel wreath, on high suspended,
> That is to crown our name when life is ended.

In his letter to Haydon of May 10, 1817 he writes, 'The Trumpet of Fame is as a tower of Strength, the ambitious bloweth it and is safe'. We can see, then, that desire for fame was intimately entangled with Keats' urge to write. Other references bear this out, but these early ones have special point in showing that this made part of his first determination to give his life to poetry as a vocation, and helped to sustain his creative enthusiasm.

After *Why did I laugh* Keats' attitude to fame and poetry changed completely. In the serial letter which included the sonnet he wrote,

> I am still at a stand in versifying—I cannot do it yet with any pleasure—I mean however to look round on my resources and means— and see what I can do without poetry.

and in a letter posted on June 9th we find,

> I have been very idle lately, very averse to writing; both from the
> overpowering idea of our dead poets and from abatement of my love
> of fame.

We can be sure that the change came at once, for in the same serial
letter that includes *Why did I laugh* on April 30th he copies out two
sonnets on fame. Here is the crucial one:

> How fever'd is that Man who cannot look
>   Upon his mortal days with temperate blood,
> Who vexes all the leaves of his Life's book
>   And robs his fair name of its maidenhood;
> It is as if the rose should pluck herself,
>   Or the ripe plum finger its misty bloom,
> As if a clear Lake meddling with itself
>   Should cloud its pureness with a muddy gloom.
> But the rose leaves herself upon the Briar
>   For winds to kiss and grateful Bees to feed,
> And the ripe plum still wears its dim attire,
>   The undisturbed Lake has crystal space—
> Why then should man teasing the world for grace
> Spoil his salvation by a fierce miscreed?

Keats says in this sonnet that the man who does not live easily as
the rose, taking life and circumstance as they come is fevered (not
sane in fact). He is like a clear lake that cannot leave itself in peace
but must stir itself up. Why then should man spoil his salvation by a
'fierce miscreed'? Both 'fierce' and 'miscreed' are strong words. A
creed is a basic belief that one lives by. In his *Ode on Indolence* he
refers to ambition as

>   pale of cheek,
> And ever watchful with fatigued eye;

showing how he had felt driven by it.

    Keats' own clarification of his sonnet precedes it immediately in
the letter where he quotes it, although the composing of the sonnet of
course came first. He is developing the experience of *Why did I laugh*
and expounding the new philosophy of life induced by it. He now
sees a purpose in pain, and unhappiness as necessary and essential. He
says that even if men could be happy, life would still end in death.
So that

> The whole troubles of life which are now frittered away in a series
> of years, would then be accumulated for the last days.

Thus the pains of life gradually prepare us for death. We experience its deprivation piece-meal and so by easier stages than if death came suddenly to end a life of bliss. In any case, he says, he does not believe we can find a way to be happy in life, 'the nature of the world will not admit of it—the inhabitants of the world will correspond to itself'. So he suggests it is better to look at life as a vale of Soul-making, this being its purpose. He says we are all intelligences, but we have to make ourselves souls. Men are 'not Souls till they acquire identities, till each one is personally itself'. This is 'modern' indeed. Many psychologists, professional and amateur are now hammering that nail home. Keats continues by saying that the best medium for doing this is precisely the world we have. It has three materials,

> the Intelligence—the human heart (as distinguished from, intelligence or Mind) and the World or Elemental space suited for the proper action of Mind and Heart on each other for the purpose of forming the Soul or Intelligence destined to possess the sense of Identity. . . . Do you not see how necessary a World of Pains and troubles is to school an Intelligence and make it a Soul? A Place where the heart must feel and suffer in a thousand diverse ways. Not merely is the Heart a Hornbook. It is the Mind's Bible, it is the Mind's experience, it is the text from which the Mind or Intelligence sucks its identity. As various as the Lives of Men are—so various become their Souls, and thus does God make individual beings, Souls, Identical Souls of the sparks of his own essence.* . . .   . . . If what I have said should not be plain enough, as I fear it may not be, I will put you in the place where I began in this series of thoughts—I mean I began by seeing how man was formed by circumstances—and what are circumstances but touchstones of his heart? and what are touchstones but provings of his heart, but fortifiers or alterers of his nature? and what is his altered nature but his Soul?—and what was his Soul before it came into the world and had these provings and alterations and perfectionings?—An intelligence without Identity—and how is this Identity to be made? Through this Medium of the Heart?—and how is the heart to become this Medium but in a world of Circumstances?

This was written between April 15th and 30th. On the 30th he says he has just written the sonnet on fame. If we apply this thinking to it, then fame appears as a fierce miscreed, a mistaken madness driving the poet, when he ought to live like a rose without letting ambition drive him, finding his salvation or soul through alterations in his attitudes induced by circumstances.

* In Jung's terms, the individuation process.

I think we must conclude, therefore, that the agonizing point of the conflict that troubled Keats in the period of depression that preceded *Why did I laugh,* although it probably arose out of his realization that he might never win fame and a bad conscience over Isabella, was the discovery that his one purpose in life was to gratify himself—that what made him a poet was the desire for fame, and that his love was entirely self-interested. These two pillars on which his ego-desires, his ego-strength most rested were undermined at once. It must have been as though his whole world fell in ruins. On the ground so cleared he built this new philosophy of life, which fitted and gave significance to his experience.

A study of the attitude of artists of all sorts to the desire for fame would be interesting. Milton's categoric statement about it will be remembered :

Fame is the spur that the clear spirit doth raise
(That last infirmity of Noble mind)
To scorn delights, and live laborious dayes :

This driving force of fame may be related to the pride that the man seeking a spiritual consummation finds his 'last infirmity'. Both differ from all other sins (for selfishness is not among the deadly sins) in being what I have called ego-pillars. They are forms of selfishness, but with a special character as 'last infirmities'. The other deadly sins like greed, malice, and lusts of the flesh are not ego-props. One who gives way to these undermines his ceativeness or spirituality, but not so with ambition or pride until the other sins have been overcome. Perhaps the creator, who by definition suffers inroads from his unconscious, needs the prop of ambition to strengthen his ego, so that he may withstand pressure from the unconscious. The prospective saint, also, may need pride. They may need them as supports in order to sacrifice everything else to the one desire. This may explain the strange unconsciousness of Keats until now of the nature of his desire for fame. It explains how he could hold disinterestedness as the virtue he chiefly admired, and by implication of his criticism of his friends when they showed signs of lacking it, felt himself to possess, and yet unashamedly acknowledge how much his creativeness depended on intense self-interest—a desire so exorbitant that it asked for the perpetuation of his works long after his death.

A phrase in this letter stands out in view of Keats' earlier statements that the poet is a man with no identity. Here he says that men are not souls till they acquire identities, till each one is personally himself. Keats' newly found knowledge of his own base motives has given him a sense of self-discovery. He now knows himself, knows what his identity is. He discovers himself to be by no means a merely passive and sensitive receptacle for divine intimations but as self-regarding as the commonest of men. He has acquired this knowledge not passively as an incursion from a beyond of wisdom, but by perception of what he himself actually is like. It is a realization of his own nature, and therefore of his own identity. And since this realization was followed at once by a sense of peace, a feeling of calm sanity, he had at the same time a sense of the wholeness of the Self. He realized his own identity as based on the Self. As one realization he became aware of his identity as a distinct ego different from any other ego and of his Self. His experience was not one of losing himself in an archetypal world, or of being dazzled by contact with it to such an extent that he felt he had no identity, but of having differentiated his ego from his Self, and realized both in wholeness.

This development of Keats' personality did not harm his creativeness, apart from taking away the desire for fame as an urge to write. Indeed this crucial letter goes on to include his *Ode to Psyche*, which is not merely the first of his great odes, but according to his own statement the first poem he wrote as an artist. He says of it,

> The following Poem—the last I have written—is the first and the only one with which I have taken even moderate pains. I have for the most part dash'd off my lines in a hurry. This I have done leisurely—I think it reads the more richly for it, and will I hope encourage me to write other things in even a more peaceable and healthy spirit. You must recollect that Psyche was not embodied as a goddess before the time of Apuleius the Platonist who lived after the Augustan age, and consequently the Goddess was never worshipped or sacrificed to with any of the ancient fervour—and perhaps never thought of in the old religion—I am more orthodox than to let a heathen Goddess be so neglected—

This is to say it was written with a new consciousness, and is less driven by unconscious forces. This would allow him to write with more judgment, which is a conscious activity. The *Ode to Psyche* is interesting from the psychological point of view, since here for the first time he puts the Self before poetry as his goal. Up to now it has been hidden within poetry as the goal. The ode is so significant as chronicling his new attitude that I shall quote it in full:

O Goddess! hear these tuneless numbers, wrung
    By sweet enforcement and remembrance dear,
And pardon that thy secrets should be sung
    Even into thine own soft-conched ear:
Surely I dreamt to-day, or did I see
    The winged Psyche with awaken'd eyes?
I wander'd in a forest thoughtlessly,
    And, on the sudden, fainting with surprise,
Saw two fair creatures, couched side by side
    In deepest grass, beneath the whisp'ring roof
    Of leaves and trembled blossoms, where there ran
        A brooklet, scarce espied:

'Mid hush'd, cool-rooted flowers, fragrant-eyed,
    Blue, silver-white, and budded Tyrian,
They lay calm-breathing on the bedded grass;
    Their arms embraced, and their pinions too;
    Their lips touch'd not, but had not bade adieu,
As if disjoined by soft-handed slumber,
And ready still past kisses to outnumber
    At tender eye-dawn of aurorean love:
        The winged boy I knew;
But who wast thou, O happy, happy dove?
        His Psyche true!

O latest born and loveliest vision far
    Of all Olympus' faded hierarchy!
Fairer than Phoebe's sapphire-region'd star,
    Or Vesper, amorous glow-worm of the sky;
Fairer than these, though temple thou hast none,
    Nor altar heap'd with flowers;
Nor virgin-choir to make delicious moan
    Upon the midnight hours;
No voice, no lute, no pipe, no incense sweet
    From chain-swung censer teeming;
No shrine, no grove, no oracle, no heat
    Of pale-mouth'd prophet dreaming.

O brightest! though too late for antique vows,
    Too, too late for the fond believing lyre,
When holy were the haunted forest boughs,
    Holy the air, the water, and the fire;
Yet even in these days so far retir'd
    From happy pieties, thy lucent fans,
    Fluttering among the faint Olympians,
I see, and sing, by my own eyes inspir'd.
So let me be thy choir, and make a moan
    Upon the midnight hours;
Thy voice, thy lute, thy pipe, thy incense sweet
    From swinged censer teeming;

Thy shrine, thy grove, thy oracle, thy heat
Of pale-mouth'd prophet dreaming.

Yes, I will be thy priest, and build a fane
In some untrodden region of my mind,
Where branched thoughts, new grown with pleasant pain,
Instead of pines shall murmur in the wind :
Far, far around shall those dark-cluster'd trees
Fledge the wild-ridged mountains steep by steep;
And there by zephyrs, streams, and birds, and bees,
The moss-lain Dryads shall be lull'd to sleep;
And in the midst of this wide quietness
A rosy sanctuary will I dress
With the wreath'd trellis of a working brain,
With buds, and bells, and stars without a name,
With all the gardener Fancy e'er could feigh,
Who breeding flowers, will never breed the same :
And there shall be for thee all soft delight
That shadowy thought can win,
A bright torch, and a casement ope at night,
To let the warm Love in !

The poem takes shape to reflect the new state of consciousness that Keats has arrived at, although it has features adumbrated even in *Endymion*. The scenery has a similarity with that in *Endymion*. The poet finds the goddess in a forest, suddenly; she was couched with Love in deepest grass beneath a roof of whispering leaves and 'trembled' blossoms mid flowers hushed and cool, in the dawn of love. But she is presented as a new goddess he has never met before, and in particular he says she is fairer than any of the old goddesses, fairer than Phoebe, the great goddess of *Endymion*, the goddess of poetry. Since at least part of *Hyperion* is in Keats' background too, we may take it that his stressing that she comes after the old hierarchies means that she is felt by him to represent a fresh development of his own soul. She is in fact the modern goddess—the goddess of the twentieth century too, for she is the Self. This becomes patent in the stanza where he says he will build a fane to her. It not only has imagery suggesting the Self, but suggests that Keats is speaking of his late experience. He says his thoughts are newly grown, and moreover with pleasant pain. He will, he says, build in an untrodden part of his mind and therefore with new self-knowledge. The shrine will be in the heart of wild country with trees clustering darkly and ringed with mountains, thus in the centre of a mandala. He calls the place a 'wide quietness'. In this it resembles the Cave of Quietude. He will build it with his working brain and with his imagination. Its birds and bells are without a name and therefore not yet identified by consciousness. The gardener Imagination never repeats; he is the discoverer of new images; none of his flowers recur in the same form. And the shrine will be bright with the ancient torch of consciousness, the torch being the symbol for a religious light that shines from the unconscious depth of the Self. There will be an open window to let Love, the God, come in. All this shows that the *Ode* describes his new state of consciousness, and refers to the Self.

Although one may build a fane for the Self, one cannot command its entry. What I am going to suggest in the next chapter is that the *Ode to a Nightingale* was written to clarify a meeting with the Self not in imagination, or by means of intuitive imagery, but as an overwhelming experience.

ODE TO A NIGHTINGALE

I

My heart aches, and a drowsy numbness pains
   My sense, as though of hemlock I had drunk,
Or emptied some dull opiate to the drains
   One minute past, and Lethe-wards had sunk:
'Tis not through envy of thy happy lot,
   But being too happy in thine happiness,—
      That thou, light-winged Dryad of the trees,
         In some melodious plot
      Of beechen green, and shadows numberless,
         Singest of summer in full-throated ease.

II

O, for a draught of vintage! that hath been
   Cool'd a long age in the deep-delved earth,
Tasting of Flora and the country green,
   Dance, and Provençal song, and sunburnt mirth!
O for a beaker full of the warm South,
   Full of the true, the blushful Hippocrene,
      With beaded bubbles winking at the brim,
         And purple-stained mouth;
      That I might drink, and leave the world unseen,
         And with thee fade away into the forest dim:

III

Fade far away, dissolve, and quite forget
   What thou among the leaves hast never known,
The weariness, the fever, and the fret
   Here, where men sit and hear each other groan;
Where palsy shakes a few, sad, last gray hairs,
   Where youth grows pale, and spectre-thin, and dies;
      Where but to think is to be full of sorrow
         And leaden-eyed despairs,
      Where Beauty cannot keep her lustrous eyes,
         Or new Love pine at them beyond to-morrow.

IV

Away! away! for I will fly to thee,
   Not charioted by Bacchus and his pards,
But on the viewless wings of Poesy,
   Though the dull brain perplexes and retards:
Already with thee! tender is the night,
   And haply the Queen-Moon is on her throne,
      Cluster'd around by all her starry Fays;
         But here there is no light,
      Save what from heaven is with the breezes blown
         Through verdurous glooms and winding mossy ways.

V

I cannot see what flowers are at my feet,
    Nor what soft incense hangs upon the boughs,
But, in embalmed darkness, guess each sweet
    Wherewith the seasonable month endows
The grass, the thicket, and the fruit-tree wild;
    White hawthorn, and the pastoral eglantine;
        Fast fading violets cover'd up in leaves;
            And mid-May's eldest child,
The coming musk-rose, full of dewy wine,
      The murmurous haunt of flies on summer eves.

VI

Darkling I listen; and, for many a time
    I have been half in love with easeful Death,
Call'd him soft names in many a mused rhyme,
    To take into the air my quiet breath;
Now more than ever seems it rich to die,
    To cease upon the midnight with no pain,
        While thou art pouring forth thy soul abroad
           In such an ecstasy !
Still wouldst thou sing, and I have ears in vain—
    To thy high requiem become a sod.

VII

Thou wast not born for death, immortal Bird !
    No hungry generations tread thee down;
The voice I hear this passing night was heard
    In ancient days by emperor and clown :
Perhaps the self-same song that found a path
    Through the sad heart of Ruth, when, sick for home,
        She stood in tears amid the alien corn;
            The same that oft-times hath
Charm'd magic casements, opening on the foam
    Of perilous seas, in faery lands forlorn.

VIII

Forlorn ! the very word is like a bell
    To toll me back from thee to my sole self !
Adieu ! the fancy cannot cheat so well
    As she is fam'd to do, deceiving elf.
Adieu ! adieu ! thy plaintive anthem fades
    Past the near meadows, over the still stream,
        Up the hill-side; and now 'tis buried deep
            In the next valley-glades :
Was it a vision, or a waking dream ?
    Fled is that music :—Do I wake or sleep ?

CHAPTER FOUR

I DO not take the nightingale of the *Ode* to be a symbol, an image trailing untellable meanings, but an actual bird. The poem is addressed not to *the* nightingale, the symbol of the nightingale, or the idea of it, but to *a* nightingale, one particular bird.

Keats may not have been what today is called a bird watcher, but he certainly observed birds. In *I stood tip toe* we find

> Sometimes goldfinches one by one will drop
>   From low hung branches; little space they stop;
> But sip, and twitter, and their feathers sleek;
> Then off at once, as in a wanton freak :
> Or perhaps, to show their black, and golden wings,
> Pausing upon their yellow flutterings.

The *Imitation of Spenser* has,

> There the king-fisher saw his plumage bright
> Vieing with fish of brilliant dye below;
>   . . . .
> There saw the swan his neck of arched snow,
> And oar'd himself along with majesty;
> Sparkled his jetty eyes; his feet did show
> Beneath the waves like Afric's ebony.

In the epistle, *To my Brother George* comes,

> I see the lark down-dropping to his nest,
> And the broad winged sea-gull never at rest;
> For when no more he spreads his feathers free,
> His breast is dancing on the restless sea.

The lark in lines *Written on the day that Mr. Leigh Hunt left prison* is 'sky-searching' and in *To a Friend who sent me some Roses* it shakes 'the tremulous dew From his lush clover covert'. In Book I of *Endymion* Keats refers to 'The chuckling linnet' with 'its five young unborn', to 'a wren light rustling Among sere leaves and twigs', and 'the nested wren . . . beneath a sheltering ivy leaf', to 'the speckled thrushes' and 'the space Of a swallow's nest-door'. Among his later verse, *Fancy* has

>   hark !
> 'Tis the early April lark,
> Or the rooks, with busy caw,
> Foraging for sticks and straw.

I take 'early' to mean early in the day, for April is not early in the year for the lark to sing. Some of these references have biological details like the clover field where the lark nests and the linnet's five eggs. We cannot miss the bird-nesting boy in some of them.

Keats was as familiar with nightingales. Nightingale-woods surrounded the old mansion at Enfield, where he was at school. Nevertheless in his early poems literary influences contaminate his references to them; they betray his immaturity. In one of his feeblest efforts, *To some ladies* we find,

> Ah! you list to the nightingale's tender condoling,
> Responsive to sylphs, in the moon-beamy air.

which is like verse on an Irish post-card. Nearly as bad from *On receiving a curious shell, and a copy of verses from the same ladies* comes,

> There, oft would he bring from his soft sighing lute
> Wild strains to which, spell-bound, the nightingales listen'd;

Nothing could be more unreal unless Keats' very young attitude to 'ladies'. *Calidore* does better with, 'Deaf to the nightingale's first under-song', and at the end of the poem, 'Clear was the song from Philomel's far bower'. The epistle *To George Felton Mathew*, puts them in their real habitat:

> covert branches hung,
> 'Mong which the nightingales have always sung
> In leafy quiet:

In the sonnet *To one who has long been in city pent*, among the joys of the country he places 'Catching the notes of Philomel'. *Sleep and Poetry* has the bird-nesting touch:

> More secret than a nest of nightingales?

and cancelled lines of *Endymion* 'the Nightingale's complain Caught in its hundredth echo'. From *Hyperion* I have already quoted,

> The nightingale had ceas'd, and a few stars
> Were lingering in the heavens, while the thrush
> Began calm-throated.

Bards of Passion and of Mirth refers to its song as 'Not a senseless, tranced thing'. In *St. Agnes Eve* we find,

> As though a tongueless nightingale should swell
> Her throat in vain, and die, heart-stifled, in her dell.

I need not illustrate further except to bring to mind from references that precede the *Ode* the one that comes nearest to being a symbol. I have already discussed it. It occurs where Endymion suggests that the love that emanates from the Self may bless the world with

> benefits unknowingly;
> As does the nightingale, upperched high,
> And cloister'd among cool and bunched leaves—
> She sings but to her love, nor e'er conceives
> How tiptoe Night holds back her dark-grey hood.

Here Keats uses a real bird as a simile for what may have a symbolic meaning, if I may put it like that. But it is not a symbol as Blake uses symbols or as those in dreams are. Such symbols have no reality outside the dreamer's mind; at least their 'substance' is psychological. But Keats' nightingale is 'upperched high, and cloister'd among cool and bunched leaves'. The concrete epithet, 'bunched' proves its noun not a pure symbol. Keats' bird sits on a concretely-imaged tree and retains its reality whatever its archetypal significance. Where sense-images have unconscious accretions they retain their objective reality. A real nightingale taking glory from the archetypal world is not a symbol, and a poem about it involves a different psychology from writing pure symbols. They have some relationship of course. Thus one can easily see why the nightingale should be a dream symbol for the Self. Singing in the dark and quiet of night from the heart of a wood, it does in external reality what the symbol of the Self does in inward experience. The parallel is exact. And apart from its environment the nightingale's unexpected long-drawn-out note, seemingly unrelated to its loud chirruping and quite unlike the whistle one is accustomed to from a bird, startles one as if it emanated from a world of mystery. It is surprising that Keats nowhere refers to this note. Coleridge describes it in his poem to *The Nightingale* as 'one low-piping sound more sweet than all', although 'sweet' seems an inadequate epithet for it, and Coleridge misses the mystery.

A comparison between Coleridge and Keats may throw Keats into focus. Coleridge reports extraverted observation of an actual bird. He is writing realistically. It stimulated thoughts, such as

> That should you close your eyes, you might almost
> Forget it was not day !

and that the song is joyous since 'In Nature there is nothing melancholy'. It is as if his preconceived theories about joy and nature had shut his mind to a direct apprehension of the particular quality of the nightingale's song, for it is the combination of ecstasy with a heart-rending quality that makes it startle the imagination. It has not startled Coleridge. His sense-impression does not carry a mystery as sense-impression tends to for Keats. On the other hand Coleridge's archetypal writing has a wholly unearthly quality. *The Ancient Mariner* and *Cristabel*, particularly part I, never really touch earth. Not only have the ship and the ocean in

> As idle as a painted ship
> Upon a painted ocean.

never existed except in imagination, even

> still the sails made on
> A pleasant noise till noon,
> A noise like of a hidden brook
> In the leafy month of June,
> That to the sleeping woods all night
> Singeth a quiet tune.

—even this is a thing wholly of the imagination. The brook and the sleeping woods seem shadows caught up into the air from the earth rather as if seen through blue atmosphere from an areoplane. On the other hand when Keats writes mythologically as in *Endymion* and *Hyperion* the myth is invaded by archetypal-laden sense impressions. His only mythological poem where this does not happen is the short one, *La Belle Dame Sans Merci*, which stands out as an exception. This can be realized if we put beside Coleridge:

> when, upon a tranced summer-night,
> Those green-rob'd senators of mighty woods,
> Tall oaks, branch-charmed by the earnest stars,
> Dream, and so dream all night without a stir,
> Save from one gradual solitary gust
> Which comes upon the silence, and dies off,
> As if the ebbing air had but one wave:

These are real oaks that have caught the imagination in their branches; Keats' imagination has started from experience of sense reality wherever it may lead him.

In writing the *Ode to a Nightingale* Keats was doing something new. Hitherto he had merely recollected experiences of the nightingale as incidentally relevant. Thus its giving way to the thrush may signify dawn, or it can stand for the most beautiful of songsters. But in the *Ode* he records one special experience of it. That he writes of one special experience of its song and does not use it to illustrate or indicate or symbolize something else is obscured because he describes neither the bird nor its song as Coleridge did. Their minds work differently. Keats refers only to its 'full-throated ease'. Other birds sing with full-throated ease, although perhaps not with quite such a full-throated quality. It is full-throated because its sings loudly and also possibly because its throat is full of a varied and continuous song. Thus the phrase implies an ecstatic quality. It was this ecstatic quality that moved Keats. But this is the only reference in the poem to the actual bird. It is not extraverted recollection. But this does not mean that Keats had not been deeply moved by one particular actual bird. Strictly speaking the *Ode* was written not about a nightingale, but about the poet's experience of its song. It brings to our attention that experience, rather than the bird. And only his introverted treatment obscures its origin in a sense experience.

Recent work on the *Ode to a Nightingale* has been directed to finding literary sources for it. Even Coleridge's poem has been suggested as one. But to do this is to allow oneself to be bemused quite as much as to see Burton as the source for 'Beauty is truth, truth beauty'. We have seen that Keats' impulse to creation came rather from the inward experience of his developing psyche than from his reading, although influences from his reading have their place, and that sense experience stirred his imagination. But before I go on to examine the *Ode* I had better deal with one of the suggested sources that threatens to bemuse.

Keats wrote the *Ode* sitting in the garden at Wentworth Place on April 30, 1819 during a very early spring—a spring so early that it already had some of the characteristics of summer. Brown tells us that he had enjoyed the song of a nightingale that nested in the garden. Although some doubt exists of Brown's authenticity in general, I cannot see why we should doubt that Keats writes of one particular experience. April 30th is not too early for the nightingale. It arrives in mid-April and sings at once. We know that he walked across Hampstead Heath with Coleridge on April 11th, which is rather early for its song, and that one of the themes Coleridge expatiated on was nightingales. We also know that in his series of lectures which he had given in January and February, and which Keats attended, Hazlitt talked about the nightingale in Dryden's version of *The Floure and the Lefe*, a medieval poem attributed to Chaucer. It has been suggested that Coleridge's talk or Hazlitt's comments accounts for the impulse that projected the *Ode*. Very likely Coleridge had Hazlitt in mind in his talk. Keats was already familiar with the medieval poem that Dryden translated and may have read it in Dryden's version after the lectures or after his talk with Coleridge, although there is no direct evidence for this. But if the *Ode* was about the medieval nightingale, or inspired by it one would have expected this to appear in his poem. The contrary is the fact. In stanza IV where he refers explicitly to the medieval poem, he does so as something different from his experience. He says he will fly to poetry in preference to Bacchus to recapture the ecstasy he has just experienced from listening to the nightingale that inspired his poem. And he says he will fly to poetry rather than to a nightingale in a poem, for he does not mention any nightingale at all, but the moon, and this is significant and important to his meaning, as I shall now show.

The theme of the medieval poem is not the nightingale, however important the part it plays—an allegoric rather than a symbolic one. The full title of Dryden's translation is *The Flower and the Leaf, or, the Lady in the Arbour—A Vision*. The poet, quite unlike Keats, views the bird objectively, looking for it in 'narrow mazes' 'pressed by fairy feet', and finds it at last in 'The sacred receptacle of the wood', a place never observed before, 'though oft I walked the green'. It was laid with 'well-united sods' within a 'fragrant brier' hedge. The bower had been 'built for Oberon'.

> I looked and looked, and still with new delight;
> Such joy my soul, such pleasures filled my sight :
> And the fresh eglantine exhaled a breath,
> Whose odours were of power to raise from death.
> Nor sullen discontent, nor anxious care,
> E'en though brought thither, could inhabit there :
> But thence they fled as from their mortal foe;
> For this sweet place could only pleasure know.

Here the goldfinch and the nightingale compete, and the nightingale wins the contest. The poet makes an excellent list of its particular qualities :

> So sweet, so shrill, so variously she sung,
> That the grove echoed, and the valleys rung :

The poem continues,

> And I so ravished with her heavenly note,
> I stood entranced, and had no room for thought;
> But, all o'erpowered with ecstacy of bliss,
> Was in a pleasing dream of paradise :
> At length I waked and looking round the bower,

125

> Searched every tree, and pried on every flower,
> If any where by chance I might espy
> The rural poet of the melody :
> For still methought she sung not far away :
> At last I found her on a laurel spray.
> Close by my side she sat, and fair in sight,
> Full in a line, against her opposite;
> Where stood with eglantine the laurel twined :
> And both their native sweets were well conjoined.

The poet like Keats was ravished by the song, transported into paradise with no room for thought, and felt the change back to normal consciousness as an awakening, but in contradistinction, looked round to find where the bird was and discovered it opposite her rival on a laurel spray. The birds make part of the allegory for they are partisans of opposite ways of living, and the poem is an evaluation of these two contrasting attitudes to life. After the nightingale has proved her superiority in song there appears 'A fair assembly' of nymphs dressed in white who dance and sing. The poet watches this fairy vision, and comments,

> O'erjoyed to see the jolly troop so near,
> But somewhat awed, I shook with holy fear.

The story continues with a joust of the knights of the rival factions also dressed in white. Each side has their ladies with their queen. After the nightingale's side wins, they all 'danced by star-light and the friendly moon'. Then the poet,

> inquisitive to know
> The secret moral of the mystic show,

asks its meaning from a lady of the nightingale's faction. She replies that it 'was all a fairy show', and explains that they were once human beings but as they are 'not yet prepared for upper light', till doomsday they 'wander in the shades of night'. Each May day they celebrate as the poet has seen. 'At other times' they post 'through the skies' following the moon. She continues,

> The sovereign lady of our land is she,
> Diana called, the queen of chastity :

Flora, queen of ease and loose delights, reigns over the opposite party and lost the contest. Incidentally Keats' Flora does not stand for an opposite philosophy from that of the nightingale, nor does morality of any sort appear in his Ode.

Since Keats wrote a sonnet on the medieval *The Floure and the Lefe*, certainly by March, 1817 two years before he wrote his *Ode*, we have his first impression of it:

> This pleasant tale is like a little copse:
> The honied lines do freshly interlace
> To keep the reader in so sweet a place,
> So that he here and there full-hearted stops;
> And oftentimes he feels the dewy drops
> Come cool and suddenly against his face,
> And by the wandering melody may trace
> Which way the tender-legged linnet hops.
> Oh! what a power hath white Simplicity!
> What mighty power has this gentle story!
> I that for ever feel athirst for glory
> Could at this moment be content to lie
> Meekly upon the grass, as those whose sobbings
> Were heard of none beside the mournful robins.

What impressed him was the sweet place where the scene was set, and of all things he noted which way the tender-legged linnet hopped. In particular he was moved by its white simplicity—white because of the moon and white-clad fairies dancing in moon and star-light and also because of Diana, the chaste. It relaxed him rather than excited, making him feel meek and content. He felt he could sleep like the Babes in the Wood, whose sobbings none but the robins heard. It was therefore a simple and innocent thing. But of the nightingale and any idea of ecstasy, nothing. This impression is not modified by his reference in the *Ode*. There, after he has asked for a draught of wine to enable him to recapture the ecstasy of the nightingale's song and found it inadequate to shut out the misery he expresses in the third stanza, he says he does not need Bacchus for he will fly on the viewless wings of poetry to the pain-free bliss he pines for. And it is not the nightingale of the medieval poem he refers to but the Queen Moon, Diana on her throne, clustered round by all the starry fays of the poem, who 'followed her' and avoided the day. He recollects the rule of Diana, one of heavenly unsullied beauty, a paradisial vision of light, of 'white simplicity', untouched by human misery. I take this to be the relevant quality of the poem for him, and its relevance in the *Ode* as a place where he tries to recapture the joyous world of the nightingale where misery has no place. To confuse it with the nightingale of the poem is to miss its whole significance. Keats' poem deals with agony as well as bliss. His impression of *The Floure and the Lefe* is of innocent moon-lit happiness. 'But here,' he adds, where he actually stands as he hears the nightingale of the *Ode*, here there is no light. His situation is different from that in the poem, for while the poem was flooded by white light, it is so dark where he stands that he cannot see what is at his feet, and what was at his feet was actual vegetation, not vegetation recollected from the medieval poem, however similar. The scented darkness with violets fading in the leaves and the musk-rose of mid-May already coming may record the actual fact of his situation when he heard the song, for in a letter to George, ended three days after he wrote his *Ode*, he says:

> This is the third of May, and everything is in delightful forward-ness; the violets are not withered before the peeping of the first rose.

The confusion of the two nightingales occurred first because it was not realized till recently that the reference to 'Poesy' in stanza IV was to any one particular poem rather than to poetry in general. First impressions tend to remain even when the justification for them has been undermined. And secondly there was confusion because he says he will fly to 'thee', the nightingale of his actual experience by way of poesy, just as he thought of flying to it by way of Bacchus. The undoubted resemblances between the two poems are merely co-incidental, or result from inherent aspects of the nightingale's song and its habitat. Even verbal echoes like the occurrence of the word 'sod' in both though with different associations, even if they are indeed echoes, have not suggested his meaning; that lies deep in his fresh experience. To say that Keats got his theme from the old poem would be like linking the *Ode on a Grecian Urn* with Burton because of the coincidence that beauty and truth are correlated in both.

The *Ode to a Nightingale* itself is the best evidence both of the previous experience that I suggest underlies it and of its original impact on his mind. It expresses a feeling of life as woeful experience. Into this misery has come an ecstasy. So it is written in a context of acute opposites. The *Ode* is woven of these, and within its framework comes their resolution. It is, in fact, a record of this resolution. A poet does not really choose to write such poetry. Its content germi-nates in the unconscious, and when some occasion opens a way for it, it floods into consciousness. This being so, we must look for the theme of the poem just below the threshold of consciousness. We can deduce from it, as I hope to show by cumulative evidence, that an experience of an actual nightingale's song had constellated an ecstatic awareness of the Self. If hearing an actual nightingale's song had brought him an experience of the Self, it must in the nature of the case, have been too overwhelming to be grasped by his conscious mind. The poem would then express the making conscious of what remained just below the threshold after what must have been a shattering experience. The argument for this lies in the details of the poem, which I shall now consider.

The opening stanza describes shock. It describes Keats' physical reaction to listening to the song. His heart aches and his body feels numb; he feels as if he had drunk an opiate. But it is not only his body that registers abnormally. He is aware of a lowering of the threshold of consciousness, as if he were sinking into the deepest unconscious—the deepest unconscious since not only does Lethe involve utter forgetfulness of the past and the crossing to an immortal awareness, it comes from the mythology of ancient Greece. We saw that when Oceanus, the god from an older generation than Neptune entered the underwater palace of *Endymion* he came as from a remoter unconscious, that Keats had a sense of comparative remoteness in time indicating comparative depth of unconsciousness. Therefore what he says in his opening stanza is that he has received an ecstatic manifestation from the deepest unconscious so intense that it gave him a physical shock.

Physical shock makes one side of intense experience for Keats. His body registered experience violently in this way. We must not take 'My heart aches' to be metaphorical. Keats experienced on his pulse, and indeed presumes this as an essential concomitant of intense feeling. In *The Pot of Basil* the young lover determines to reveal his first love to his lady and

all day
His heart beat awfully against his side;
And to his heart he inwardly did pray
For power to speak; but still the ruddy tide
Stifled his voice, and puls'd resolve away—

Keats' imagination is stirred by the situation of the over-excited heart making speech impossible. That is part of the drama. Similarly in *The Eve of St. Agnes* Porphyro's emotion 'in his pained heart Made purple riot'. As he watched Madeline kneel in prayer he grew faint. 'Anon his heart revives.' Of Madeline he says,

But to her heart, her heart was voluble,
Paining with eloquence her balmy side;

So we must not think this medical detail an unpoetic opening. Poets are the last people to separate experience into the prosaic and the poetic. Keats does not keep medical observation shut away from his imagination. Thus when the ghost in *The Pot of Basil* leaves Isabella by dissolving, he left

> The atom darkness in a slow turmoil;
> As when of healthful midnight sleep bereft,
> Thinking on rugged hours and fruitless toil,
> We put our eyes into a pillowy cleft,
> And see the spangly gloom froth up and boil :

Keats' own fevered experience of 'The atom darkness in a slow turmoil' when he buried his face in the pillow and saw the 'spangled gloom froth up and boil' has remained in his memory to glow with an imaginative quality. Thus he would not think it inappropriate to express ecstasy by means of a medical observation. The numbness that he experienced is of this sort too, for in the first version he wrote a 'painful numbness' distinguishing it from the lassitude he chronicles in the letter quoted in my last chapter as a pleasant sensation short of faintness. An observation in a letter to Reynolds in the August following the *Ode* is relevant.

> My own being which I know to be becomes of more consequence to me than the crowds of Shadows in the shape of men and women that inhabit a kingdom. The soul is a world of itself, and has enough to do in its own home. Those whom I know already, and who have grown as it were a part of myself, I could not do without : but for the rest of mankind, they are as much a dream to me as Milton's Hierarchies. I think if I had a free and healthy and lasting organization of heart, and lungs as strong as an ox's, so as to be able to bear unhurt the shock of extreme thought and sensation without weariness, I could pass my life very nearly alone though it should last eighty years.

The experience Keats comments on in his *Ode* was one of those shocks of extreme sensation. It will be remembered that he uses 'sensation' of inner impact, and that impacts from actual outer objects which he felt to be beautiful tended to stir up inner sensations or achetypes. Experience of that nature and that dimension is obviously what he refers to in the first stanza of his *Ode*—the shock of an extreme sensation in the world of the soul.

Just as the *Ode* opens by describing a lowering of the threshold of consciousness and a feeling of shock at an incursion from the unconscious, so it ends by describing the return to normal awareness. Critics who have failed to note that Keats is describing an experience and not a bird could not escape observing that the nightingale does not sing as it flies from valley to valley. But Keats was quite as aware of this as they are. Anyone who has heard a nightingale knows that it sings perched on a tree. This is not a biologist's observation but everyone's. That Keats should say the song fades out from valley to distant valley shows that he is not thinking of the bird but of his experience. And this is precisely the way a dream experience does fade out, like a sound receding into the distance. Keats characterizes the experience further as something indescribable, and incomprehensible. 'Was it a vision,' he asks, 'or a waking dream?' We must take his questions as literally as his opening statement that his heart ached. He has experienced something quite out of this world, the closest definition for which he finds as either a vision or a dream experienced when he was awake. How better could he describe an experience of the Self as an awake experience? Not only so. How can his question make sense if he is not indeed speaking of just this?

Of the other details in the first stanza I need not say much. Keats experienced the nightingale's song when in a depressed mood, as we see from his saying that it was not envy of its happier lot that made his heart ache. This statement may also be necessary to make it unambiguous that to say his heart aches is not a metaphor for saying that he is unhappy. I do not attach great importance to his calling the nightingale a Dryad. This is a very literary way of calling it a woodland spirit, being almost a *cliché*. In the first draft of the poem he referred to it as a 'Small winged Dryad'. 'Small winged' shows that he has the bird in mind, not a nymph. It sings of summer in ecstasy. Keats was particularly sensitive to the weather. Summer weather made him joyous, as rain depressed him. We have already seen that the structure of *The Eve of St. Agnes* is formed on the plan of winter and cold spelling misery, and the 'southern' moors escape from it. Moreover the winter just gone had Tom's death at its core, and now a wonderful early summer seemed beginning. Singing of summer in ease is like singing of a land where snow and hail never fall and there is always a soft air, singing of Elysium, the paradise beyond Lethe.

The first stanza of the *Ode* described the impact of the nightingale's song. Stanzas II and III, which belong together, trace the experience into less profound awareness. Provençe, imagined as a land of dance and song and sunburnt mirth is less deeply buried in the unconscious than the Elysium beyond Lethe. Keats describes a surfacing consciousness in these stanzas. By the third he has reached the painful prose reality of his own everyday experience. Stanza II bridges the gap from the depth to ordinary awareness. Not only is imagery from Provençe nearer to Keats than that from Greek mythology, but the intensified experience of intoxication is less deeply in the unconscious than that of the waters of Lethe. Emergence from the archetypal to the familiar makes the tension between the opposites of ecstasy and despair apparent. It is not merely, however, that the intense quality of the third stanza comes from Keats' personal experience of misery. Only to think, that is to say, only to be thoroughly aware is to be full of 'leaden-eyed despairs'. This is the general condition of life. Its misery is heavily enough weighted to raise the scale against the ecstasy he has experienced, and is not felt as bathos but as contrast. Moreover it does not destroy the significance of the ecstasy, but stands in opposition to it.

Perhaps I should say something more about Keats' asking for wine to recapture the ecstasy, although I have already shown its relevance. He follows it up in stanza IV by saying he will fly to the nightingale not charioted by Bacchus, but on the viewless wings of poetry, since poetry has the stronger wings, and is the more potent intoxication. He already observed this in *Hence Burgundy, Claret, and Port* quoted in his letter to Reynolds of January 31, 1818. There he said that since he is a poet, the wine which he drinks in preference to these, is that received through his eyes and is brighter and clearer. This is an old fancy of his. The *Ode* therefore makes no confirmation of Gittings' argument that the depression he had just gone through drove him to drink. I think Gittings' argument thin. It is in any case irrelevant here. The poem could not suddenly spring from stanza I to stanza III. It needed a transition. And Keats' transition glows with sunburnt abandon, where wine 'With beaded bubbles winking at the brim' is a delight of the awakened imagination not one of stupor.

Of stanzas IV and V I have already said enough. Before it was realized that the reference is to *The Floure and the Lefe*, it was inexplicable, but now involves no difficulty.

Stanza VI opens by emphasizing his situation of listening in the dark. Remembering his recent discovery of death as the solution of life's fretful experiences and the reward, he comments, 'Now more than ever seems it rich to die'. Keats is never far from the actualities of life. It would not be rich to die as Tom did. He qualifies his statement by 'To cease upon the midnight with no pain'. Perhaps he heard the nightingale at midnight and this merely records closeness to that fact. Or he may have in mind his midnight illumination of

Why did I laugh. If he died now it would be 'rich', for it would be to die in the greatest fullness of experience, when the song would be a 'high requiem' although he became a sod unaware of it.

Gittings gives a mundane association of ideas for the appearance of the word 'requiem'. Keats had been reading Burton's *Anatomy of Melancholy* which contains this:

Bacchus et afflictis requiem mortalibus affert.

He had just written on Bacchus and here is the association. But there is no association of *ideas* at all. Keats is not referring to the *requiem* that Bacchus gives afflicted mortals, but to a 'high requiem', the mass for the dead. The poem takes a turn at this stanza. Up to now he has been describing the impact of the song and his attempt to remain in its ecstasy while in fact surfacing from it. He begins again, meditating as he listens in the dark. What he writes now is a reverie—something less buried in the unconscious than the experience was. He therefore uses modern words for the mystery. The song is a 'high requiem', a 'plaintive anthem', neither Lethean nor Bacchus-induced, nor poetry induced. He considers his position relatively to the experience of the song. He compares it with that of similar experiences. He says he has often been in love with easeful Death. But now it seems more than ever rich to die. This has been the richest of all such experiences. Death would have a new quality now, for if he died now he would do so in a peace made by that experience, a peace made *for him* by it, for a requiem is a mystery sung not for a congregation but for the one soul. Although he would be a sod, unaware and worthless, he would die in that peace. The stanza expresses his awareness of his mortal ego's relationship with the immortal Self, which will sing peace to it when it has become utterly unaware, for the Self does not depend on consciousness. The song will give him a peace within which he can sleep in death for ever.

If I were to say that much senseless criticism had been written about the next stanza it would not be an intemperate statement. Critics, even a poet who should have known better, have said silly things about it. If we take it as referring to the actual nightingale, or to a generalized nightingale, whatever that would be, then it makes no sense. All critics who make sense of it perceive that Keats is addressing something immortal, the immortal in himself as has been best said. The immortal in oneself is the Self. In fact the stanza makes sense only if one presumes that the *Ode* was written to the Self as constellated for Keats by listening to a nightingale. In stanza

VI he presented his ego-attitude within the Self, his relationship to it from the ego-angle, and he said he could find everlasting rest in it. In his stanza he considers it not from the ego-angle, but as it were from the archetypal. He tells us what *it* is. The ego is fleeting and mortal, but the Self is everlasting. One cannot, of course, know what the attitude of the Self is, just as one cannot know what God is. So he addresses the Self, and says what the ego intuits of its nature. It is ecstatic utterance. Ecstatic utterance is the only one adequate for addressing the Self. But it is also no more than precise analysis. And I shall discuss it as precise analysis of the truth of the Self. Let me quote it so that its ecstatic quality, its essential quality can speak first.

> Thou wast not born for death, immortal Bird!
> No hungry generations tread thee down;
> The voice I hear this passing night was heard
> In ancient days by emperor and clown:
> Perhaps the self-same song that found a path
> Through the sad heart of Ruth, when, sick for home,
> She stood in tears amid the alien corn;
> The same that oft-times hath
> Charm'd magic casements, opening on the foam
> Of perilous seas, in faery lands forlorn.

The archetypal Self exists untouched by the misery of soul-starved generations—body-starved too no doubt, for Keats nowhere in the poem forgets the actual situation of himself and of mankind in the created universe, and there was much starvation in the England of his day, but even more soul-starved than body-starved. Its voice is heard by emperor and poor man indifferently. It is the same voice the poet has heard this passing night as has always sung. He moves from his own hungry generation back in time and in his own consciousness to the past, then deeper into his own consciousness where it sings in the sad heart of Ruth.

We ask why Ruth? The answer to that I doubt if we can know for certain. In a joking passage in a letter to Tom of July 3, 1818, where he writes of the Scottish Church and thrift having 'done Scotland harm' and of Burns, 'poor unfortunate fellow' having in reality a Southern disposition and being deadened by his Scottish upbringing, he adds,

> It is true that out of suffering there is no dignity, no greatness, that in the most abstracted pleasure there is no lasting happiness. Yet who would not like to discover over again that Cleopatra was a Gipsy, Helen a rogue, and Ruth a deep one?

It is difficult to deduce from this frivolity what Ruth meant to him. She certainly makes one of his three archetypal women. Cleopatra and Helen stand out in literature as what in Jungian psychology would be called *anima* types—the sort of women who attract men's love, and in their effect bring ruin and tragedy, though Jungians do not need to subscribe to this effect as inevitable. What stands out as serious in Keats' joke is that all three must have their shadow side. But he does not inform us of their positive significance, unless it can be taken as the opposite. Then Ruth would mean for him simple disinterested goodness. Perhaps we should be content with the aspect of Ruth that appears in the poem, her home sickness in a foreign land. If the voice is to sing to emperor and clown, it must also sing in women, and as the whole feeling of the poem is of this ecstasy bursting out in a world of sadness, perhaps Ruth, as she already existed in his mind as one of the great types of womanhood, was his obvious choice. Certainly Cleopatra and Helen would not convey his meaning. Ruth is a type of perfect woman, suffering not only through no fault of her own, but through deliberate self sacrifice and loyalty. Her suffering is undeserved and therefore both most poignant and most indicative of the nature of the world, apart from this ecstatic song. Moreover she is alone and homesick and in an alien land, and man's spiritual home which he feels deprived of and alienated from is his Self. If we say that Ruth is an *anima* figure of Keats', then we can also say that she is his own soul, and that what he has now said is that this song of the Self sings actually within his own soul, which is suffering from its own home sickness.

This leads Keats on to the further statement that the song has often charmed magic casements opening not only into the faery lands of the unconscious where it belongs but into a mystery beyond all possibility of consciousness. In fact Keats here refers to the deepest awareness of the Self that man can have, when he feels pouring into it a breath from beyond experience, from beyond creation—a mystery perhaps even beyond the Self, that the Self opens a window into. Garrod made an illuminating suggestion of the association that might have led Keats to think of Ruth. He suggested that it echoes from Wordsworth's *The Solitary Reaper*—not that Wordsworth mentions Ruth, but that he writes of a girl reaping corn and singing. I should guess that the real association in Garrod's mind, not in Keats', was that Wordsworth was moved as Keats was by a song out of mystery. Wordsworth's reaper sang in solitude. Her song filled the whole valley, 'the Vale profound'. He asks who will tell him what she sings, and comments,

> No Nightingale did ever chaunt
> More welcome notes to weary bands
> Of travellers in some shady haunt,
> Among Arabian sands :
> A voice so thrilling ne'er was heard
> In spring-time from the Cuckoo-bird,
> Breaking the silence of the seas
> Among the farthest Hebrides.

People who like verbal explanations, as I do not, may say the associative word is 'nightingale'. The furthest Hebrides, the *ultima Thule*, have from the earliest history stood as the last land in the sea which encircled the known world. From them one looked out on a mystery beyond knowledge. Wordsworth's experience comes very near to Keats'. The song of the solitary reaper has the inner quality of Keats' nightingale. It stirred the poet more deeply than he could fathom. He heard in it a note from beyond itself. Both poems catch an echo from the furthest reach of man's consciousness. But Keats is the more aware of what he hears. Wordsworth suggests that she may sing of 'old, unhappy, far-off things, And battles long ago'. Keats already had experiences nearer to it. He ended his *Ode to Psyche* by saying he would build a shrine to the goddess with 'a casement ope at night, To let the warm Love in !'—a window to let the invisible God enter. The experience of the nightingale took him further than this. The casement of the *Ode to a Nightingale* looks out on seas that are utterly unknown, where no guess finds anything to seize on.

The next stanza brings the experience down to earth. Keats has explored his experience to the furthest and now returns to normal awareness. It is done with a flash of creative insight. The connecting experience relating the two worlds is 'forlorn'. 'Forlorn' has two different meanings. 'Lorn' is the old past participle of 'lost', and 'for' an obsolete prefix that intensifies the word following it. So 'forlorn' means utterly lost, utterly unknowable. The other meaning is the familiar one of being utterly miserable. The one meaning applies to the furthest limits of inner experience, the other to that of everyday living. Keats says the word tolls him back like a bell tolling for death, the loss of that moment of immortality. The nightingale's song was his inner requiem, and this connecting link tolls him back to his sole self. His sole self is his ego (his usual meaning for the word 'self'). In the first book of *Endymion*, as I need hardly remind anyone, after referring to 'that moment' when we have

136

> stept
> Into a sort of oneness, and our state
> Is like a floating spirit's.

he continues,

> But there are
> Richer entanglements, enthralments far
> More self-destroying,

where 'self' certainly means ego. Later he comments, when Endymion is exhausted by the wonders in the landscape of Dian's temple and sits down

> There, when new wonders ceas'd to float before,
> And thoughts of self came on, how crude and sore
> The journey homeward to habitual self !

The meaning of the word 'ecstasy' implies an out of the body, out of the ego experience so there is nothing startling in Keats' statement that after ecstasy one has to return to one's habitual self. But what is interesting here is his use of the adjective 'sole'. An experience where the ego is lost in the Self, or to use Keats' words for his early experience 'destroyed' is a much less conscious one than that when the return is described as to 'habitual self'. A return to one's habitual self implies an experience where the ego was not 'destroyed' or lost in the Self, but merely in an unfamiliar situation. Return to the 'sole self' implies that the ego had been in an even fuller and richer relationship with the Self. It implies an experience of the ego within its larger environment. Only then can the return to habitual self be called return to the 'sole self', the separated self. It is interesting that Jung defines consciousness with no more precision than Keats' as an awareness that is separate.

I have already examined the implications of the last words in this stanza, as referring to the fading out of the experience. The third and fourth lines,

> Adieu ! the fancy cannot cheat so well
> As she is fam'd to do, deceiving elf.

may refer to stanza IV, to his going to *The Floure and the Lefe* to recapture the ecstasy, or it may be a reference to his own poetry, to the reverie he has just described. Alas, he says, poetry cannot capture and hold this ecstasy. Poetry is a deceiving elf because she seems to promise this, but she cannot fulfil her momentary 'imitation' of it.

This stanza makes the necessary anticlimax to the poem. The poet returns to his sole self, poetry cannot keep him in perpetual ecstasy, that music of the nightingale is fled. The lines about poetry being a deceiving elf have been taken as a repudiation of all poetry as false escapism, and in particular as a repudiation of the ecstasy of the nightingale's song. Such criticisms are interesting as showing how impossible it is to understand poetry by thinking it. Something more than thought is required to understand. The experience of the nightingale's song was a reality—a reality experienced for too short a time. That an experience comes to an end does not mean it never was. Keats does not repudiate it. Indeed how could he, or anyone who has read the poem with imaginative understanding. He began his *Ode* by referring to an experience so extreme that it was felt as a shock. He tried to hold it, to perpetuate it. But, he considered, intoxication will not do so, but poetry will. Then he stood in the dark meditating. For a moment he indeed recaptured something of the mystery. In the end, however, he must let it go. The Self cannot be captured. Not even poetry, however promising the attempt, can do this. It has its moment, but the moment ends. This coming down to earth and noting that the ecstasy cannot be perpetuated makes part of the experience itself. The *Ode* records an unearthly experience, an invasion into consciousness of something quite beyond familiar experience—so beyond that it is incredible, unimaginable until experienced. 'Fled is that music', says Keats. He comments on it as something gone, not as something that never was.

CHAPTER FIVE

IN a process, what follows may throw light on what precedes, indeed sometimes even seem to account for it, as the fruit interprets the flower. The odes following that to a nightingale show fruitage. Thus the *Ode on a Grecian Urn*, but perhaps only because of 'Beauty is truth, truth beauty', has appeared as the culmination of something. The statement certainly sums up something in a concept. From one of his letters we saw that Keats had arrived at the conclusion that philosophy is to poetry as truth to an eagle, which I take to mean that the concepts of a philosopher in his sense of the word, are intellectualizations of experience. I take it that for Keats the relationship of truth to beauty is the same. Thus the summing up in the *Ode on a Grecian Urn* is a sort of tautology. Beauty for Keats was entangled with intimations of the Self. I have suggested that a nightingale's song brought what might be called an invasion of the Self into his consciousness. The Self has the quality of irreducibility: it cannot be translated into anything else. It is the furthest reach of experience and therefore of knowledge. Keats might well intellectualize this as truth, which is then also a permanent and irreducible reality. If this is a fair description, his statement about truth and beauty means that beauty, not objects of beauty, but the experience of them, what gives them the quality that moves, their intimations of the Self, is the final unchangeable, indubitable reality. Conversely this unchangeable, irreducible reality is what gives objects of beauty their quality. Therefore his statement neither needs further elucidation nor can receive it. It cannot be argued by logic, for it presupposes an experience felt on the pulse, and logic does not depend on verification by the pulse. The statement is no more than an acceptance of the experience that inspired the *Ode to a Nightingale*. Keats' next sentence follows even by logic: that is all he needs to know, or that we need to know if we accept experience as being prior to logic. To prove by logical means gives a deeper satisfaction to the thinker, and may indeed be necessary for him, but logic is not relevant to an understanding of Keats, whose value judgment is made without it, since it is a feeling one.

The *Ode on Melancholy*, also written in May shortly after the experience of the *Ode to a Nightingale*, is another fruit. Keats writes not in despair but with melancholy. His attitude to the pain of life has changed. Until now he has found the Self in an environment of misery. The Cave of Quietude was surrounded by 'Dark regions'; it was a quietude in our 'native hell'. After the experience of *Why did I laugh* he thought of misery as a preparation for death, and indispensible for the creation of souls. But now he presents it as something to be desired. And it is to be sought not in Lethe since drowning in unconsciousness prevents 'the wakeful anguish of the soul'. It 'dwells with Beauty—Beauty that must die:'

> Ay, in the very temple of delight
> Veil'd Melancholy has her sovran shrine,

This means not that misery has the Self at its core, as he once had experienced, but that the Self has misery within it. This makes a notable step in his acceptance of it, and in consciousness. Joy and misery are twin opposites. Just as in *Endymion* he said that only those who experience Hell find the Cave of Quietude, so here he says that only those who experience joy at its extremity know what Melancholy is. Melancholy, he says at the climax of his ode is

> seen of none save him whose strenuous tongue
> Can burst Joy's grape against his palate fine;
> His soul shall taste the sadness of her might,
> And be among her cloudy trophies hung.

So sadness has been taken into the mystery of the Self. It has become an archetypal figure, no longer the concrete facts of the young dying of consumption, or the old groaning their life away, but a goddess with her shrine. It has become one of that goddess's wonders. It is 'veil'd' and hung among 'cloudy' trophies, since it comes from a depth of consciousness wrapped in the Self's impenetrable mystery.

In this ode Keats is saying something different from what he says in the *Ode on a Grecian Urn*. The urn is like a frozen archetype. It is a permanent object passed from generation to generation of sorrowing humanity, but has fixed on it objects of beauty. The song of the nightingale had not this frozen objective permanence. Its permanence lies in the realm of the psyche. It is captured for a moment by sorrowing men and women of each generation. Melancholy does not attach to the urn, but lies in the quality of fleetingness that makes an essential aspect of man's ecstatic awareness of the Self. Keats could reach an intellectual concept in the *Ode on a Grecian Urn* because he contemplated a frozen archetype, and his contemplation included a moment when imagination turned into thought. But the archetypes of the odes on melancholy and to a nightingale are living energies.

To complete this study I must follow up Keats' changed attitude to his muse. This results from the experience not so much of the *Ode to a Nightingale* as from that of *Why did I laugh*. The *Ode on Indolence* is relevant and may make a good link with what I said in Chapter III, particularly as I should date it before the *Ode to a Nightingale* since the three figures on its urn, Love, Ambition and Poetry, are those referred to in the letter ending on May 3rd. He says there that Poetry, Ambition and Love 'seem rather like figures on a Greek vase', objects outside himself, no longer having any relevance to himself. As we so often find comments in a letter resulting from poetry just written, this makes a good reason for placing the ode between *Why did I laugh* and the *Ode to a Nightingale*. On the other hand it should be said that he refers to the *Ode on Indolence* in a letter written to Miss Jeffrey with a postmark of June 9th following. He says he has 'been very idle lately'

> both from the overpowering idea of our dead poets and from abatement of my love of fame. I hope I am a little more of a Philosopher than I was, consequently a little less of a versifying Pet-lamb. I have put no more in Print or you should have had it. You will judge of my 1819 temper when I tell you that the thing I have most enjoyed this year has been writing an ode to Indolence.

'The versifying Pet-lamb' appears in the *Ode on Indolence* as 'A pet-lamb in a sentimental farce!' But in this letter he refers not to poetry written lately, but to poetry written in 1819. Indeed the comparison with other writings in 1819 suggests others written since. If my dating is right, the *Ode on Indolence* is likely to have been written in the relief that followed the experience of *Why did I laugh* and not to be the last of his series of odes, as is commonly supposed. Its whole tone corresponds with the letter that ends on May 3rd.

This letter included *La Belle Dame Sans Merci* among other verse that would probably convey more to a depth psychologist than is apparent to the inexpert amateur. La Belle Dame is presented as a female demon who bewitches the 'wretched wight', betraying him and leaving him 'Alone and palely loitering' where 'The sedge is wither'd from the lake, And no birds sing'. I accept the general impression that La Belle Dame personifies poetry, or Keats' muse. The *Ode on Indolence* differs from *La Belle Dame* in expressing relief from the influence of his 'demon Poesy', and the pressure of ambition. It expresses the conscious mood of his letter. It would seem therefore

141

that *La Belle Dame Sans Merci* represents a more unconscious reaction to his experience, the sense of bitter wrong done him by her domination, or by the loss he now experiences. She has cheated him by her promise, exhausted him and left him in a barren land with dried up imagination since no birds sing, and with no impulse to do anything but loiter in a desolate world. Whether or not, however, my dating is right, the letter of June 9th continues the mood of March 13th. It shows that the urgency has gone from his creative impulse now that fame has lost its virtue. The influence of the dark experience behind *Why did I laugh* was not temporary. It altered his attitude to his muse irretrievably.

Since Keats continued to write some of his best poetry after that experience, this means that what poetry he now wrote came out of a changed purpose. It may indicate that he found a deeper source for his writing. The experience was followed almost at once by the *Ode to Psyche* and the *Ode to a Nightingale*. We have seen that in the *Ode to Psyche* he for the first time put Psyche or the Self as a superior goddess to Phoebe, his first muse. The *Ode to a Nightingale*, if my interpretation can stand, expresses an experience of the Self, and the odes on a *Grecian Urn* and on *Melancholy* are poems about the Self. His allegiance has shifted. We can see the fruitage of this in poetry he was now to write. The negative attitude to poetry that resulted from the experience of *Why did I laugh* along with his positive experience of the Self of the nightingale-experience introduced a divided attitude to himself as a poet. His old muse being superseded involved a new judgment on his work. We can see a repercussion in *Lamia*.

Lamia resembles La Belle Dame, and his 'demon Poesy'. She belongs to a class of demon muse. Keats says of her,

> She seem'd, at once, some penanced lady elf,
> Some demon's mistress, or the demon's self.

A philosopher destroys her hold on Lycius, and this has been held to show that Keats wrote to condemn philosophy as a destroyer of poetry. But I think this is too superficial a judgment both because Lamia represents only his old muse now superseded, and also because what he means by philosophy needs to be recollected.

I shall deal with philosophy first as it is the easier. Keats always had a great respect for philosophy. In the early days he admired Bailey as being a philosopher, when he thought of himself as not being at all philosophical. Later he seemed to feel that his development occurred in this direction. He developed, however, not by feeling less, or being less of a poet, but by gradually knowing or understanding what he felt. He never repudiated the feeling that for him necessarily preceded his thought. He said, with *Endymion* in mind, that the value of philosophy, or understanding, or knowledge, was that it prevented one being blown sky high or hither and thither by one's feelings, not that it destroyed them. He felt that philosophy steadied his poetic feeling. Apollo at the end of *Hyperion* becomes a god, that is to say a poet, the god of poetry, because through agony he came to knowledge of his experience; that is to say by becoming a philosopher. Keats described the agony that preceded *Why did I laugh* as the agony of ignorance. The philosophies he then developed in his letters dispelled ignorance. What he means by the truths of philosophy is illustrated in the *Ode on a Grecian Urn*, a wisdom from intuitive perceptions that emerge from 'soul'-experiences.

One must be careful about how much one takes *Lamia* to be an allegory. In the first place it is a story in the sense that *The Pot of Basil* is a story, moreover a story retold without alteration. He found it ready-made in Burton's *Anatomy of Melancholy*. His writing of it was therefore a process of a different sort from that of *Endymion* or of *Hyperion*, or even from that of *The Eve of St. Agnes*, for *The Eve of St. Agnes* was much more the elaboration of a situation than a story. *The Eve* has no knot to be developed or untied. The hero merely walks into a castle belonging to his enemies and carries off the lady of his dream. It happens as a result of nothing and nothing results. Thus it is not surprising that its structure should be determined by the nature of the Self, or that it says much more than is apparent. It takes a shape that was already imprinted on Keats' mind, a track he already knew, that of the Self as a core of light and warmth and love in an opposite environment. The structure of *Lamia* on the other hand is precisely that of Burton's story with the sole addition of an introduction. Therefore any special significance Keats gives to his story must be looked for there.

The introduction to *Lamia* is indeed significant. It opens with a somewhat parallel story to that of Lycius, happening to a god. Lamia enables Hermes to find the invisible nymph he loves, by breathing on his eyes and letting him see her. He wins his desire and Keats comments,

> It was no dream; or say a dream it was,
> Real are the dreams of Gods, and smoothly pass
> Their pleasures in a long immortal dream.

Keats made this comment on the dreams of the gods in *Endymion*. And he makes it here to signify a difference from that of the dreams of mortals. Lycius' dream was not real. That makes the point of the story. Apollonius put an end to indulgence in an unreality.

The introduction makes Keats' attitude to Lamia clear also. He judges her false. She is a dream-maker, and as a muse, false. She was

> Not one hour old, yet of sciential brain
> To unperplex bliss from its neighbour pain;
> Define their pettish limits, and estrange
> Their points of contact, and swift counterchange;

Since it was Keats' experience that this cannot be done, that pain and joy belong inevitably together, by saying this he presents her as a deceiver. She is, however, a creature of wonderful beauty, a serpent of many colours in many designs, perhaps scintillating light since she is lustrous. But there is no indication that he thought of her as having any connection with the Self, which he might have done, for the mythical Lamia has some such significance. Keats feels her to have a beautiful, but false fascination, like La Belle Dame Sans Merci.

I have suggested that the experience behind *Why did I laugh* revealed to Keats the ego-centredness of his muse, and that just as this led to his devaluing of fame, so also did it lead to his devaluing his muse. But it led also to his finding a new allegiance. He expressed this first in the *Ode to Psyche*. It and all the other great odes are inspired by his new goddess, the Self. They come out of such profound experience that the old muse of poetry seems by comparison a deceiving elf, a betraying demon, a false fascination. That Keats contrasts the dreaming of Lycius with Hermes' immortal dream seems to say the same thing. The archetypal dream is real and immortal, but to think that poetry inspired by a muse that presents unalloyed happiness and perfection as a reality of the sub-lunary world is false. To fall under the fascination of Lamia, the false muse, leads to the same destruction as to be kissed four times by La Belle Dame Sans Merci.

Keats seems to have been puzzled by La Belle Dame kissing her knight precisely four times. He makes light play with his question in the letter where he quotes it. He gives as his answer,

> because I wish to restrain the headlong impetuosity of my Muse—she would have fain said 'score' without hurting the rhyme—but we must temper the Imagination as the Critics say with Judgment. I was obliged to choose an even number that both eyes might have fair play, and to speak truly I think two a piece quite sufficient.

Suppose I had said seven there would have been three and a half a
piece—a very awkward affair and well got out of on my side—

This is as much as to say that he did not know. He then goes on
immediately to write some extempore verse called,

Chorus of Faeries ~~three~~ 4 Fire, air, earth, and water—

If the unconscious knows more than the conscious mind, the answer
may lie there. It certainly favours rhyme, and is probably responsible.
Four is the number that represents the Self. Keats' immediately thinking of a chorus of the four elements (which talking at the mythological level made up the Self no less than the stuff of the external
universe) seems to indicate that the lady knew what she was about
and that the muse of poetry enthralled Keats because she indicated
that she had the Self in her pocket. This is born out by evidence
already supplied. Thus it may not be fanciful to see a symbol of his
attitude in 'three' (perhaps representing ambition, poetry and love)
scored out and '4', the four elements of the Self, put in its place. This
study of Keats certainly suggests that he first dedicated himself to
poetry because he felt that it held the secret of life, which he later
discovered to be the Self. The *Ode to a Nightingale* shows his mind
on a swivel. His first instinct, when he tried to maintain the ecstasy
of the Self, was his old one of going to poetry, his strongest intoxication, to recapture it. But although he did by means of it in fact recapture for his readers all that was possible, he makes a judgment against
it. Fancy is a deceiving elf and cannot do this. It was by this trick
that La Belle Dame with her four kisses had deceived him, led him
astray and landed him in sterile desolation. Not only so, he had
discovered her ego-centred limitation, her league with ambition. He
now realizes that she has cheated him. Lamia is that cheat.

On the level of prose the story of *Lamia* is even more sinister. It is
one that must always have been 'modern'. I knew a young woman
of eighteen who spent a week alone with a phantom lover in lodgings
in London, and when her father at length found her, refused to return
to the world of prose. Oddly enough she too was a poet at her own
level, and a student. I was her tutor. At this level Keats tells his story
with great discernment. And at this level, no less than on a deeper
interpretation, Lycius feels guilty whenever the world of reality
threatens to break in, for he is guilty. The story begins with Lamia
lying in wait for him. She slides into his consciousness during an
absent-minded reverie, when he is in the twilight of the shades of
Plato, his mind 'shut up in mysteries', in the region where thoughts

are not clear and 'reason fades'. In dreary indifference he comes towards where she waits, and passes her without noticing, but she calls him to look at her, and when he does, it is as if he already loved her. He addresses her as a goddess with all power. She says she is a real woman and loves him.

> Lycius from death awoke into amaze.

He rightly judged that a real woman is better than any goddess. Once he has accepted her as real, he is in her power. She takes control at once. He walks back to Corinth with her quite unaware of his surroundings.

> The way was short, for Lamia's eagerness
> Made, by a spell, the triple league decrease
> To a few paces; not at all surmised
> By blinded Lycius, so in her comprized.
> They pass'd the city gates, he knew not how,
> So noiseless, and he never thought to know.

When they meet his tutor Apollonius in the street, Lycius shrinks 'Into his mantle'. He goes to live in a dream palace until the loud sound of trumpets disturbs his phantom-life.

> Lycius started—the sounds fled,
> But left a thought, a buzzing in his head.
> For the first time, since first he harbour'd in
> That purple-lined palace of sweet sin,
> His spirit pass'd beyond its golden bourn
> Into the noisy world almost forsworn.

But

> The lady, ever watchful, penetrant,
> Saw this with pain, so arguing a want
> Of something more, more than her empery
> Of joys; and she began to moan and sigh
> Because he mused beyond her, knowing well
> That but a moment's thought is passion's passing bell.

And not passion's alone.

When Lycius tries to bring her into real life and invites guests to his wedding, she remains in her palace and turns out to have no contact with reality at all; she has no relations, no friends to invite to her marriage. But she prepares an even more gorgeous setting for the feast. In Keats' story the guests enter the phantom palace with amazement. Apollonius comes uninvited and looks around with his ruthless observation.

146

> The bald-head philosopher
> Had fix'd his eye, without a twinkle or stir
> Full on the alarmed beauty of the bride,
> Brow-beating her fair form, and troubling her sweet pride.

Lamia turns icy cold and eventually fades away, and Lycius dies of shock. That is the end of the story. The contrast between Hermes' immortal dream and Lycius' is complete. The poem distinguishes between the archetypal fact that is immortal, and the phantasy that cannot persist in the world of cold prose reality.

It is not, however, that this poem is anything so crude as an allegory showing that philosophy kills poetry. Lycius is a philosopher in Burton's story. Consequently his tutor Apollonius is a philosopher too. It is not philosophy but contact with reality that destroys the dream, both in Burton and in Keats. Nevertheless Keats expresses his dramatic sympathy for his hero, duty bound at least, by his much quoted lines;

> Do not all charms fly
> At the mere touch of cold philosophy?
> There was an awful rainbow once in heaven:
> We know her woof, her texture; she is given
> In the dull catalogue of common things.
> Philosophy will clip an Angel's wings,
> Conquer all mysteries by rule and line,
> Empty the haunted air, and gnomed mine—
> Unweave a rainbow, as it erewhile made
> The tender-person'd Lamia melt into a shade.

This is not the philosophy that Keats respects as full awareness of reality. It describes what is still called 'Natural Philosophy' in the Scottish Universities; in other words physics, which in Keats' day no doubt dealt realistically with the rainbow, gave common things dull names and conquered 'all mysteries by rule and line', though now it has opened doors to the imagination, not to say Hell. I do not therefore think Lamia an allegory saying that philosophy kills poetry. But it does show that poetry pretending to give ecstasy unalloyed by pain, poetry that is merely a charm, fails to stand up to the test of reality. At a deeper level it shows that poetry is now something Keats has rejected in preference for the Self as the ultimate truth. In the Self, pain and joy cannot be separated. If we can take Apollonius as a personification of philosophy in Keats' usual sense for the word, which I doubt, we can say that he shows that the knowledge of experience (particularly of the Self) destroys the lesser sort of

147

poetry that sets out to supply bliss unalloyed, as reason destroys illusion.

Lamia makes a bridge for our understanding, between Keats' attitude to his muse in his first version of *Hyperion* and his second. One of the puzzling things about his introduction to *The Fall of Hyperion: a Dream* is that there he no longer speaks of himself as a poet. *Lamia* makes this intelligible. But more than this, *The Fall of Hyperion* culminates the experience begun in *Why did I laugh*. The sonnet led to his saying farewell to the three ghosts of Love, Ambition and Poetry. He does so in his *Ode on Indolence* by saying to them,

> Ye cannot raise
> My head cool-bedded in the flowery grass;
> For I would not be dieted with praise,
> A pet-lamb in a sentimental farce !
>
> — — —
>
> Vanish, ye Phantoms ! from my idle spright,
> Into the clouds, and never more return !

This, as I suggested, left him with a problem, for he continues to write poetry and yet his new allegiance is the Self. He opens *The Fall of Hyperion* with this problem. He begins by saying that

> Fanatics have their dreams, wherewith they weave
> A paradise for a sect; the savage too
> From forth the loftiest fashion of his sleep
> Guesses at Heaven;

but 'Poesy alone can tell her dreams'. Every man 'whose soul is not a clod' has dreams. Whether he himself is a poet or a fanatic

> will be known
> When this warm scribe my hand is in the grave.

During his dialogue with Moneta, who will tell him what he must write, and who therefore is his new muse, he no longer talks of himself as a poet. Moneta says,

> 'Art thou not of the dreamer tribe?
> The poet and the dreamer are distinct,
> Diverse, sheer opposite, antipodes.
> The one pours out a balm upon the World,
> The other vexes it.'

Keats then shouts out in spleen,

'Apollo ! faded ! O far flown Apollo !
Where is thy misty pestilence to creep
Into the dwellings, through the door crannies
Of all mock lyrists, large self worshipers
And careless Hectorers in proud bad verse.
Though I breathe death with them it will be life
To see them sprawl before me into graves.
Majestic shadow, tell me where I am,
Whose altar this; for whom this incense curls;
What image this whose face I cannot see,
For the broad marble knees; and who thou art,
Of accent feminine so courteous?'

Keats may have thought of Hunt as the lyrist and perhaps Byron as
a Hectorer in bad verse. He had long outgrown Hunt, and he recognizes a distinction between Byron and himself. In a letter to George,
dated September 17, 1819 he says,

> You speak of Lord Byron and me. There is this great difference
> between us: he describes what he sees—I describe what I imagine.
> Mine is the hardest task; now see the immense difference. The
> Edinburgh Review are afraid to touch upon my poem. They do not
> know what to make of it; they do not like to condemn it, and they
> will not praise it for fear. . . . They dare not compromise their
> judgments on so puzzling a question.

To his admirers Keats felt he was a pet-lamb and their praising him
a sentimental farce. The real truth was, he says, that he has not the
necessary quality of a poet, which is to please. He is not, that is to
say, Lamia-inspired, not like the poet of *The Floure and the Lefe*, who
presented a happy faeryland with nymphs following the moon. But
if he is not a poet, what is this dreamer that he now calls himself? He
has rejected poetry, but here he is again dedicating himself, and
here is Moneta, a new muse again guiding him. He has taken his
way from the external world, precisely as he first did in *Endymion*,
through woods where he partakes of a feast that seemed left 'By
angel – – or our Mother Eve', just as there his hero feasted at every
new awareness of the Self. He feels the draught he drinks as 'parent'
of his theme, and when he awakes to the consciousness it brings, he
finds himself by a gigantic sanctuary. He looks all ways, north, south,
east; and to the west—a significant point of the compass—he sees
an altar. Awed, he makes towards it by the inevitable attraction that
an altar always had for him. But in this grim new region of his mind
he finds not ecstatic joys as in *Endymion*, not dawn as in the first
version of *Hyperion*, but what lies to the west, the secret of death.

This is what he wants to penetrate, the mystery he seeks to know. His new muse is a figure of veil'd terror, too terrible to endure until she raised her veil, for ignorance is still the greatest terror.

> I had a terror of her robes,
> And chiefly of the veils, that from her brow
> Hung pale, and curtain'd her in mysteries,
> That made my heart too small to hold its blood.
> This saw that Goddess, and with sacred hand
> Parted the veils. Then saw I a wan face,
> Not pin'd by human sorrows, but bright-blanch'd
> By an immortal sickness which kills not;
> It works a constant change, which happy death
> Can put no end to; deathwards progressing
> To no death was that visage; it had past
> The lilly and the snow; and beyond these
> I must not think now, though I saw that face—
> But for her eyes I should have fled away.
> They held me back, with a benignant light,
> Soft mitigated by divinest lids
> Half-closed, and visionless entire they seem'd
> Of all external things;—they saw me not,
> But in blank splendor, beam'd like the mild moon,
> Who comforts those she sees not, who knows not
> What eyes are upward cast. As I had found
> A grain of gold upon a mountain's side,
> And twing'd with avarice strain'd out my eyes
> To search its sullen entrails rich with ore,
> So at the view of sad Moneta's brow,
> I ask'd to see what things the hollow brain
> Behind environed : what high tragedy
> In the dark secret chambers of her skull
> Was acting, that could give so dread a stress
> To her cold lips, and fill with such a light
> Her planetary eyes; and touch her voice
> With such a sorrow.

Her theme is the death of the gods, as far as gods can die. Keats' approach to this new muse is through acceptance of his own death. That he has sought her, as she makes clear, leads inevitably there. Hitherto his muse has chosen him, whether as the Moon in love with the young poet casting her spell on him, or as the destructive Belle Dame. Now in spite of his knowledge of that merciless power he still makes for the altar where mystery can be partly penetrated. No wonder he asks himself what sort of dreamer he is.

The altar appeared to him to

<pre>
                        spread around
        Forgetfulness of everything but bliss.
</pre>

It is an altar 'clouded . . . with soft smoke', and he hears from its 'white fragrant curtains' a voice saying,

<pre>
                        'If thou canst not ascend
        These steps, die on that marble where thou art.
        Thy flesh, near cousin to the common dust,
        Will parch for lack of nutriment—thy bones
        Will wither in few years, and vanish so
        That not the quickest eye could find a grain
        Of what thou now art on that pavement cold.
        The sands of thy short life are spent this hour,
        And no hand in the universe can turn
        Thy hourglass, if these gummed leaves be burnt
        Ere thou canst mount up these immortal steps.'
</pre>

He feels 'the tyranny Of that fierce threat and the hard task proposed'.

<pre>
        Prodigious seem'd the toil; the leaves were yet
        Burning—when suddenly a palsied chill
        Struck from the paved level up my limbs,
        And was ascending quick to put cold grasp
        Upon those streams that pulse beside the throat :
        I shriek'd, and the sharp anguish of my shriek
        Stung my own ears—I strove hard to escape
        The numbness; strove to gain the lowest step.
        Slow, heavy, deadly was my pace : the cold
        Grew stifling, suffocating, at the heart;
        And when I clasp'd my hands I felt them not.
        One minute before death, my iced foot touch'd
        The lowest stair; and as it touch'd, life seem'd
        To pour in at the toes : I mounted up,
        As once fair angels on a ladder flew
        From the green turf to Heaven—'Holy Power,'
        Cried I, approaching near the horned shrine,
        'What am I that should so be saved from death?
        What am I that another death come not
        To choke my utterance sacrilegious, here?'
</pre>

We can see how far Keats has progressed from his first version of the story if we compare this with Apollo's death. Apollo too shrieked and became a god, but Keats himself, the mortal in touch with the immortal, asks what he is that he should be saved; he is no god. He now attributes nothing to himself; his ego is dead. But that death involves an answer to his questioning. The 'veiled shadow' replies,

> 'Thou hast felt
> What 'tis to die and live again before
> Thy fated hour, that thou hadst power to do so
> Is thy own safety;'

He asks to have his 'mind's film' purged off. She replies,

> 'None can usurp this height . . .
> But those to whom the miseries of the world
> Are misery, and will not let them rest.
> All else who find a haven in the world,
> Where they may thoughtless sleep away their days,
> If by a chance into this fane they come,
> Rot on the pavement where thou rottedst half.'

Keats says he does not understand, for he has done nothing to relieve the suffering in the world. But the voice replies that philanthropists are not the dreamers who come here. It is not to them that she refers.

> 'They are no dreamers weak,
> They seek no wonder but the human face;
> No music but a happy-noted voice—
> They come not here, they have no thought to come—
> And thou art here, for thou art less than they—
> What benefit canst thou, or all thy tribe,
> To the great world? Thou art a dreaming thing,
> A fever of thyself—think of the Earth;
> What bliss even in hope is there for thee?
> What haven? every creature hath its home;
> Every sole man hath days of joy and pain,
> Whether his labours be sublime or low—
> The pain alone; the joy alone; distinct:
> Only the dreamer venoms all his days,
> Bearing more woe than all his sins deserve.'

Moneta speaks a wisdom discovered only by those who dream; that is to say, those who live an inward life, who cannot find their home in the external world. This reminds one of the statement of Jesus of Nazareth that the foxes have holes but the Son of Man has nowhere to lay his head, which was given by Dr. Elizabeth Howes in a lecture to The Guild of Pastoral Psychology as one of the things that result when a Self is lived 'existentially, not as a hope or a vision'. It is a description of a stage in the journey of the man of unusual spiritual depth and courage, of one who inevitably bears 'more woe than all his sins deserve'. Moneta then reminds Keats (which is to say that Keats bethinks himself) of intimations of his new bliss which he has already experienced, gardens into which 'thou didst pass erewhile', temples where he suffered, like those in fact recorded in such poems as the *Ode to Melancholy*. Because of that, says Moneta, you stand safe here. Keats replies that he rejoices 'That I am favour'd for unworthiness'. This expresses the humility of those who have found their Self. It is not reached in fact by anyone who has not experienced the ego's utter failure, and therefore knows its unworthiness. So he is told that he is here because of his previous discoveries which he chronicled as a poet. But he looks round and finds no other poets in this solitude. She has spoken of 'his tribe'. What then is his tribe? What class of dreamer is he? She then gives the distinction I have already quoted between his tribe and that of the poet. In fact Keats has discovered that he is the sort of dreamer who perceives the archetypal vision and who undergoes the death of his ego. Not only so, he is one who deliberately sacrifices his ego—no, not deliberately, for he is forced to sacrifice his ego by his Self. Hence the significance of the altar in the poem. An altar is not a shrine where one worships but that on which a sacrifice is performed. Keats describes the archetypal situation represented in the Christian Churches by the mass, but he does not do so in the Christian way, which represents a sacrifice by the proxy, Christ. Jung might say by the 'projection'. He does it by a more conscious way, and therefore in a greater agony. It may be, I should say in a much greater agony. It is, too, an agony in which he risks perishing. But out of it he feels life coming into himself again. Jung interpreting the Mass says that Christ is both sacrificer and sacrificed. Here Keats describes himself as seeking death in coming to the altar. So Keats himself, or his Self is sacrificer and his ego is sacrificed. That is his choice. It is both a free choice and not a free choice. His will carries out a choice determined not by his will, but by his Self. Keats by coming to the temple of Moneta chooses to be slain, and saves himself only because he consciously and with great effort steps towards the altar himself. If he does this with all his power and arrives in time he will survive. New life pours into him from the altar steps. The altar in *The Fall of Hyperion* is therefore the place where the ego is sacrificed to the Self and Keats' new muse, Moneta, the muse of the Self. He has not only cast off the old deceiving muse (who none the less had helped him to the Self) but found his new one. After his submission to Moneta he tries to proceed with the poem, but it is Saturn that Moneta serves, the god of death, death to the ego, and there could be no creative impulse behind a poem planned to have him superseded. Keats no longer worships Apollo. It is a new sort of poetry that he feels dedicated to. He gave the poem up soon after the clarification of this introduction, and inevitably, because of this dilemma.

It is interesting to look in Keats' letters for any confirmation of his new allegiance. We have seen that he now finds his main interest in the life of the soul, which is now more to him than a 'kingdom' of 'shadows' in the shape of men and women he does not know, that is to say a reading public. It is man's function to make a soul out of his intelligence. We have seen him engaged in doing this in *The Fall of Hyperion*. If we accept the dates for his writing it as from August to October 1819, we find the tone of his letters fitting. In one to Fanny Brawne with postmark August 16th he says,

> The thousand images I have had pass through my brain—my uneasy spirits—my unguess'd fate—all spread as a veil between me and you. Remember I have had no idle leisure to brood over you—'tis well perhaps I have not. I could not have endured the throng of jealousies that used to haunt me before I had plunged so deeply into imaginary interests.

An imaginary interest that enabled him to endure jealousy must be a deeper one that just the artist's. It implies his new inward life. To Taylor on the 23rd he writes,

> You will observe at the end of this, if you put down the letter, 'How a solitary life engenders pride and egotism!' True—I know it does: but this pride and egotism will enable me to write finer things than anything else could—so I will indulge it. Just so much as I am humbled by the genius above my grasp am I exalted and look with hate and contempt upon the literary world. . . . I am not a wise man. 'Tis pride—I will give you a definition of a proud man. He is a man who has neither Vanity nor Wisdom—one filled with hatreds cannot be vain, neither can he be wise.

On August 25th he talks of his pride and obstinacy in his work. He apologizes for himself:

> It would be vain for me to endeavour after a more reasonable manner of writing to you. I have nothing to speak of but myself, and what can I say but what I feel? If you should have any reason to regret this state of excitement in me, I will turn the tide of your feelings in the right Channel, by mentioning that it is the only state for the best sort of Poetry—that is all I care for, all I live for.

The best sort of poetry is no doubt that inspired by his new muse. The objective observation of his own feelings in this letter may show that his view is not ego-confined. He writes of his hatred, his pride and his obstinacy as if they were that of someone else he was observing. He holds at the same time two contradictory views about them. He condemns his own feelings, but also permits and condones them since they serve his purpose of writing the best sort of poetry, the work that he still exists to do. This suggests a viewpoint that is not ego-centred, although it also implies an ego in pain, but not swamped by it.

About this time Keats was in his last creative flow. In this letter he noted that his body could not stand up to the strain, and that he must at times be content to stop and be nothing. It is tempting to guess what happened in his inner life after this. I seem to have written an inner biography, and it is frustrating not to be able to continue. But the basis has been his poetry. And not long after this any clear evidence ends.

What I hope I have shown in this study is that poetry fascinated Keats from his early youth because he felt it held the secret of life, that in *Endymion* he differentiated out from their entanglement his consciousness of his pursuit of beauty, his erotic feelings and his Self, that his development involved first rejecting the nature of the Hawk as essential in life and as part of his own nature, then accepting it in himself, perhaps forced to it by Fanny Brawne putting out the light of Isabella Jones and the realization of his failure as a poet, that this agony came to a head and was resolved by some sort of experience of the Self on the midnight he wrote *Why did I laugh*, than an astounding experience of the Self, as recorded in the *Ode to a Nightingale*, followed, and that the realization of his Hawk-like side involved his loss of ego-interest in ambition and poetry, but led to a clear realization of the Self as his goal, and that out of this he developed a new attitude to his vocation as a poet, where the Self took the place of the ego, and Moneta, the priestess of the death of the ego, the priestess of the Self, took the place of his old muse.

INDEX

157

GEORGE ALLEN & UNWIN LTD

London: 40 Museum Street, WC1

Auckland: 24 Wyndham Street
Bombay: 15 Graham Road, Ballard Estate, Bombay 1
Bridgetown: P.O. Box 222
Buenos Aires: Escritorio 454–459, Florida 165
Calcutta: 17 Chittaranjan Avenue, Calcutta 13
Cape Town: 68 Shortmarket Street
Dacca: 24 Topkhana Road, May & Baker Ltd, Compound, Dacca, 2
Hong Kong: 44 Mody Road, Kowloon
Ibadan: P.O. Box 62
Karachi: Karachi Chambers, McLeod Road
Lahore: Nwa-I-Waqt Building, 7 Queens Road
Madras: Mohan Mansions, 38c Mount Road, Madras 6
Mexico: Villalongin 32–10, Piso, Mexico 5, D.F.
Nairobi: P.O. Box 4536
New Delhi: 13–14 Asaf Ali Road, New Delhi 1
Ontario: 81 Curlew Drive, Don Mills
Philippines: 7 Waling-Waling Street, Roxas District, Quezon City
São Paulo: Caixa Postal 8675
Singapore: 36c Princep Street, Singapore 7
Sydney: N.S.W.: Bradbury House, 55 York Street
Tokyo: 10 Kanda-Ogawamachi, 3-Chome, Chiyoda-Ku

ENGLISH LITERATURE: VALUES AND TRADITIONS

SIR IFOR EVANS

Crown 8vo   *Clo 8s 6d net, U Book 4s 6d*

In his well-known book A *Short History of English Literature*, Sir Ifor Evans described and defined his subject; here he reflects on it. Is it possible, he wonders to trace permanent elements in such a huge and varied mass of writings? As he moves from the Anglo-Saxon Caedmon to T. S. Eliot, or from Milton to James Joyce, he finds how, in unexpected ways, the English spirit of compromise extends into her literature, along with her love and nature and interest in the individual. In poetic imagery above all the British genius seems, typically, to have found a way of making 'empiricism transcendental'. This book which had its origin during the war under the aegis of the British Council provides the reader with a stimulating passport to a very rich kingdom.

THE GENIUS OF JOHN RUSKIN

SELECTIONS FROM HIS WRITINGS

JOHN D. ROSENBERG, M.A., PH.D.

Demy 8vo   *45s net*

Today, in England and America, there is a marked revival of interest in the Victorians. No figure within the period surpasses Ruskin in magnitude of genius, modernity of message, or mystery of prose. Unquestionably he was a major author, but he has yet to find a contemporary audience commensurate with his gifts.

The cause is twofold. The sheer mass of Ruskin's works (the standard edition contains thirty-nine over-sized volumes), and the intimidating variety of subjects he wrote on have tended to ward off the kind of critical attention that, say, Dickens has attracted in recent years. At the same time, there has been no comprehensive selection from all his major works available to the modern reader.

This need is filled by *The Genius of John Ruskin* edited by John Rosenberg. His generous selections from the works of the great Victorian critic-prophet are not only eminently readable—they are surprisingly contemporary in spirit.

PARADISE OF TRAVELLERS

ENGLISH VISITORS TO SEVENTEENTH CENTURY ITALY

A. LYTTON SELLS

Demy 8vo   30s *net*

Italy in the Seincento retained her prestige as the country most advanced in the arts of civilization. She was still, with France, and prior to the formation of the Royal Society, in the van of scientific research. The Academy of St Luke in Rome was the greatest art school in the world. Scientists like Galileo, historians like Paolo Sarpi, added new lustre to her name. Venice, 'the eldest child of liberty', was still glorious and powerful. Thus it was that English students flocked in numbers to Padua and that travellers regarded a sojourn in Italy as the highlight of their experience.

Dr Lytton Sells, a graduate of Cambridge and of the Sorbonne, and sometime Professor of French in the University of Durham, is now Research Professor of French and Italian at Indiana University.

VIRGINIA WOOLF

DOROTHY BREWSTER

Large Crown 8vo   20s *net*

In a short and very readable book, Dorothy Brewster has managed to give us the benefit of her many years' study, and teaching, of the works of Virginia Woolf. She knows her material so well that, along with the essential biographical details of the novelist, she is able to recreate the atmosphere of 'the Bloomsbury Group'; in this way her book gives us a valuable insight into a very rich period of English literature, involving such figures as Leslie Stephen, Leonard Woolf, Clive Bell, Lytton Strachey, Desmond MacCarthy, Christopher Isherwood, David Garnett and others. Despite the wide area covered, the book is not superficial: those readers with a long acquaintance with Mrs Woolf's works may well find that they have to reconsider some of their ideas. For example, Dr Brewster gives evidence to show that Mrs Woolf had a definite and serious interest in politics, especially in connection with women's rights. Fond as she is of her subject, Dr Brewster can criticize unfavourably when necessary; thus she finds the novelist guilty of being caught up in woolly talk about 'the Russian soul', popular several decades ago.

GEORGE ALLEN AND UNWIN LTD